STRESS
IN THE
FAMILY:
HOW TO LIVE
THROUGH IT

Tim
Timmons

HARVEST HOUSE PUBLISHERS
Eugene, Oregon 97402

STRESS IN THE FAMILY

Copyright © 1982 by Harvest House Publishers
Eugene, Oregon 97402

Library of Congress Catalog Card Number 82-081648
ISBN 0-89081-359-0

Printed in the United States of America.

CONTENTS

INTRODUCTION

A major university study on the family concluded that the most dangerous place to be in the United States (outside of riots and war) is the American home! Home is the place where people expect to find comfort, support, and a shelter from their troubles. Instead, they find too much discomfort, little support, and a boiling pot of *stress in the family.*

Every member of the family of man is over-stressed to the breaking point: man's maleness has been squashed, woman's femaleness has been shattered, and children have been robbed of their childhood by being pressured to grow up too fast and too soon. The traditional family unit (husband and wife with their own children), which has been the foundation for every healthy society since Eve offered Adam his first apricot, is experiencing dramatic erosion. Today five out of every six families have been ripped apart and broken down into fractured family units. Instead of serving as a foundation for society to rest on securely, most families have become mounds of sand upon which society sinks, slips, and slides! Someone well said, "If you can keep your head when all about you are losing theirs, then you just don't understand the problem."

THE STRESS MESS

Western thinkers divide man into body, mind, and spirit. Physicians treat the body, psychologists and psychiatrists deal with the mind, and the clergy attend to the spirit. In the past, the three areas were most often dealt with separately, but now that we have entered the age of stress, we must deal with the whole person simultaneously. One standard medical text estimates that 50 to 80 percent of all diseases have their origins in stress. Stress-induced disorders have long since replaced infectious disease as the most common maladies of people in the postindustrial nations.[1]

Today most medical research indicates that up to 90 percent of all illness is caused by the stress of modern life. In fact, many researchers are no longer asking which diseases are stress-related; instead, they are asking how much of *every* disease is stress-related.[2] During recent years, heart disorders, cancer, arthritis, and respiratory diseases have become so prominent in the clinics of the United States, Western Europe, and Japan that they are known as "the afflictions of civilization." Their prevalence stems from poor diet, pollution, and, most important, the increased stress of modern society.[3]

The wear and tear of stress is part of the cost of living; no one can avoid it. But for most of us the price has risen too high to pay. Modern man faces more daily pressures, such as the unrelenting demands of time, than ever before in history. The effect can be devastating!

Some people are only vaguely aware of the toll that stress is taking on them. Others are acutely aware of it and have the medical bills to prove it! Things such as financial difficulties, legal entanglements, business setbacks, relational conflicts, divorce, or a death in the family are obvious sources of stress. However, not all stress arises from negative events. Positive occurrences, such as a marriage, a desired pregnancy, a promotion, an outstanding achievement, or even a simple vacation can produce stress. Both winning a lottery and getting a ticket for speeding can make your heart pound, your stomach churn, and your palms sweat. Our bodies exert themselves in much the same way to cope with both desired situations and dreaded events.[4]

Stress is a force which creates upset stomachs, gnawing fear, splitting headaches, intense grief, excessive drinking, and violent arguments. Stress dulls our memories, cripples our thinking, weakens our bodies, upsets our plans, stirs up our emotions, and reduces our efficiency. But stress also motivates us to study, encourages us to keep going when life gets difficult, spurs us to action in the midst of crises, helps us to mature, and at times makes life exciting.[5]

Not only can stress be both good and bad, but it also is quite individual. When you see your lover approaching you on the street, you will most likely experience a stress response. But if I pass the same person, I may not even skip a beat. What is stressful to one person may not in any way be stressful to another.

THE BODY'S M.O. DURING STRESS

Originally "stress" was primarily a physics term referring to the resistance factor of forces which weigh against another object, such as a bridge or wall. The term was also borrowed by the other sciences until stress has emerged as a popular psychological term for life's struggles and pressures.

Dr. Hans Selye in his classic work *The Stress of Life* defines stress as the wear and tear caused by life and the nonspecific response of the body to any demand made on it.

The body's modus operandi or manner of operation (M.O.) for defending itself against stressful situations is extremely complex. Whenever a desired or dreaded stress occurs, the mind rapidly classifies it and sets off the alarm system. The nervous system takes over immediately and makes the ncessary adjustments. The pulse rate soars and respiration is retarded. As the blood pressure rises, the heart works harder to distribute the excess supply of blood to the muscles and lungs. All processes in the alimentary canal cease, and the spleen contracts, sending its concentrated corpuscles to predesignated areas. Adrenaline is excreted from the adrenal medulla; sugar is freed from the reserves in the liver; and literally thousands of other complex procedures occur instantaneously and automatically without the individual having to give them the slightest thought. This marvelous transformation, this M.O., protects and provides for the individual in stress.[6]

THERE'S A TIGER OUT THERE

Modern man seldom faces a saber-toothed tiger, as his ancestors did. Rather, his defenses are most likely to be required for a chewing out by the boss or a score of less important situations which keep the body constantly on the alert. Thus he is an organism prepared for fight, flight, or freeze, even when nothing is happening or is going to happen. He sits stewing in his own juice—literally—consisting of excess adrenaline and other glandular secretions. The stage is set for anything from a headache to a heart attack.[7]

Many people are so sensitively attuned that it doesn't require a stress of any magnitude to set off their alarm system. It may be a thought, a person's look, a TV program, or simply a plane flying overhead. *The body's chemistry is so severely altered after its defenses are alerted that if no physical action is taken, in time various physical or emotional symptoms may occur.* It's like holding the accelerator of a car to the floor while keeping its gears in neutral or its brake on. Going nowhere, the body roars and races, using up energy and wearing out its parts.[8]

THE SOCIOLOGICAL TIME BOMB

Two American Indians were talking things over in a foxhole between air raids during World War Two. "The way I figure it," one said, "is that when they smoked the peace pipe in 1918, nobody inhaled!" In our world of sociological sabotage, more and more relationships have been breaking up and falling into the witch's cauldron, which is boiling with toils and troubles! Whether between nations, minorities, neighbors, or families, relationships are rampant with conflict and pain. Among nations (the family of man), the twentieth century has given us more wars than all of the previous centuries put together. Among families (man's family), marriages aren't working, parenting is less effective, and individuals are obsessed with self-satisfaction. *The essence of the sociological time bomb is the turmoil of relationships!*

Much of our society doesn't work anymore, so our values are much in question. We judge each other by how well we hide our emotions. We are tired of our marriages and even tired of our affairs, and our children are a burden, not so much a source of love as fear. Once a North American grew up and married the girl next door, but today he can't remember her name, so he substitutes a quickie with a stewardess he met on a plane, and rushes off the next morning to a conference in Maine. TV producers have become the priests of our society, psychiatrists its geisha girls, and where once we loved people and used things, today it is just the reverse. We are a society of winners where almost everybody feels himself a loser, where cut of clothes and make of car tell us who we are. We are a youth cult where everyone is made to feel old, a love cult where far too many feel unloved. And because we set up life so it hurts, most of us hurt a lot. Once there was pressure on people to marry, but now there is pressure to break up; divorce has become an obligatory rite of passage for those who want to grow.[9]

Relationships aren't working. We've become the masters of the surfacey relationship with all its cliches. Too many people moving too fast are set-ups for pain and defeat. We are encouraged to expect perfection, but perfection doesn't exist, so we are always a little disappointed and hold back again, hoping the next round will really be *it*. But each time we get to *it* we find that somebody took it.[10]

The sociological time bomb is perpetuated by how we handle our children. In an interview with James S. Coleman, Professor of Sociology at the University of Chicago, he commented: "I think we are becoming the first species in the history of the world which is unable to care for its young. Over all, child-rearing is one of the biggest casualties of the modern age that is being ushered in by this generation."[11]

When asked what accounts for this declining interest in children, Dr. Coleman said: "It's because the value system that used to hold families together has been turned upside down. Now the husband and wife typically put their own individual interests first, their joint goals second, and any family interests beyond the couple third. That is a reverse order from the traditional ranking that placed family concerns first and individual goals last. Because the fundamental reversal of priorities leads to more divorce and parental neglect, it has serious implications for stability of the family. Of all the changes these young adults are bringing into society, I think this breakdown of the family is going to prove to be the most powerful, the most destructive, and the most enduring."[12]

WOWERS AND WOERS

These are two general and extreme responses to the stress of life. One extreme says that life is always being on top of the pile—the *wowers*. The wower is continually "up." He's filled with "Super! Fantastic! Couldn't be better!" He virtually denies the reality of the stress around him.

The other extreme says that life is always being underneath the pile—the *woers*. The woer is overwhelmed by the stress of life to the point of being its negative, helpless victim. Instead of *exciting* people about life, the woers are *embalming* people everywhere, preparing them for death and dying. Their theme is "It won't work!"

Both of these extremes are wrong responses. Life

is not always being on top of the pile nor always being underneath the pile. *Life is full of piles!* You may be on top, underneath, attempting to go around, or preparing to shovel through! The piles of pressure and stress are unavoidable!

No matter how unavoidable stress is (because of the absolute need for survival), most people still make their attempts to avoid it. Some attempt to get rid of stress by retreating—hoping to escape it. Many try repelling it, thinking they can shield themselves from it. Others try repressing the stress, believing that somehow they can contain it within. But these avoidance techniques are only temporary at best. They move people toward eventually succumbing to destruction through stress in the family. Since we cannot avoid stress, we must learn *how to live through it*—to restore values, responsibility, relationship, maleness, femaleness, and childhood—*to recreate family!*

Stress is a killer but you can live through it!

Part One
Picture the Pressure

CHAPTER 1
Your Body's Charge Account

As I was finishing my morning run (some call it a fast walk) I encountered a growling Doberman with me on his mind. It didn't matter that I was running the last exhausting half-mile. My body's alarm system went off! I was so afraid that I wasn't sure whether to stop and talk, run faster, or attack my new acquaintance! So what did I do? I froze. Then I talked to this angry dog as if he could understand me. Just when I thought I was destined to be a snack for my new "friend," I heard the beautiful voice of the dog's owner commanding him to stop. The dog looked disappointed, I was relieved, and the owner was embarrassed. Charge this experience to my body's charge account.

The human body has a lifesaving reaction pattern for adapting or coping with pressure. This stress-response pattern is an extremely complex interplay of chemical secretions, physical functions, and electrical messages. The body's stress response to any pressure (good or bad) is like a firing or charging of all systems in preparation for fight or flight.

Whatever the pressure—a dog, a bear, the boss—your body begins its stress response. Your heart races at 100-plus beats per minute (normally 60 to

75). Your hands may become cold and clammy, and perspiration tests out your favorite deodorant. Your hands may shake and at the same time your body takes on a readiness posture, with all major skeletal muscles tense.

Internally, there is a chain of events within the structure of your central nervous system triggered by the pressure. Your sympathetic nervous system, which is one of the two main branches of the autonomic nervous system, comes fully into play and activates a virtual chemical orchestra of hormone secretions. The small portion of your brain called the hypothalamus triggers the pituitary gland, which is located nearby at the base of your brain. The pituitary gland releases its characteristic hormone, ACTH (adrenocorticotrophic adrenal glands). Located just above your kidneys, it sets off a reaction in them. The adrenals intensify their output of adrenaline into your bloodstream, along with a family of related hormones called corticoids. It is this family of hormones, but particularly adrenaline, that brings your body up to a highly aroused state. Because the bloodstream is the common communication and transport system for the entire body, these stress chemicals soon reach every cell in your body. These chemicals reach the farthest extremity in less than eight seconds. Simultaneously, commands traveling throughout your nerve pathways alert your heart, lungs, and muscles for increased action.[1]

Your body charges for action![2] Your muscles become more richly supplied with blood as the tiny blood vessels constrict and raise your blood pressure, meanwhile diverting blood away from your extremities. Your muscle tone quickly increases, making muscular action more immediate and more efficient. Your liver immediately begins working to convert its stored glycogen into glucose, which your brain and muscles need in greater supply. Your breathing becomes more rapid and intense, increasing the amount of oxygen in the blood so that your muscles and your brain can burn the glucose efficiently. Your heart pumps rapidly and intensively, sending an abundant supply of blood to those portions of your body that need it. Blood rushes to your head, and your brain's electrical activity intensifies as it optimizes its processes for conscious control of your body's actions.[3]

Your hearing becomes more acute. The pupils of your eyes dilate, making your vision more sensitive. Even the concentration of a certain clotting agent in your bloodstream increases. All in all, the stress reaction is an intricately coordinated chemical mobilization of the entire human body to meet the requirements of life-and-death struggle or of rapid escape from the situation.[4]

As you are pressured your body charges through every functional system—nervous system, cardiovascular system, digestive system, immunological system, and the skeleton-muscular system. All of this charges at about ⅛ of a second! Ready for action! It's now time for fight or flight! But most people do neither.

DEEP FREEZE

Instead of fight or flight, a very popular response to pressure is to freeze! It is important to understand that the built-in stress response in us was intended to end in *physical action*. The outpouring of sugar and fats into the blood are meant to feed the muscles and the brain so that they might *contend actively* with the stressor which has provoked the system. The dilation of the pupils occurs to give better *visibility for action* against apparent threats. The increased heart and respiration rates are to pump blood and oxygen to *active* muscles and control centers in the brain. This is not a time to sit and feel all of these sensations tearing away at the body's systems and eroding good health. This is the time to *move,* to use up the products, to relieve the body of the destructive forces of stress on a sedentary system. Appropriate activity in this case would be total body exercise, such as swimming, running, dancing, biking, or an active sport that lasts at least an hour. Such activities will use up the stress products that might otherwise be harmful and that are likely to play a part in a degenerative disease process such as cardiovascular disease or ulcers.[5]

Unlike our forefathers, who had an occasional dangerous situation or an emotional shock (*crisis stress*), it is the prolonged, unrelieved state of worry, anxiety, and arousal that many people today experience but cannot escape. The stress reaction in the body operates to mobilize for immediate action and problem-solving. But when action is not taken or cannot be taken, a continuous, unrelieved, low-level arousal is experienced without substantial relief. This is the most dangerous stressor of all—*chronic stress!*

Chronic stress is not just freezing or repressing an action response in a given situation, but a deep freeze—a freeze that can destroy you at the core of life. That's *your* life!

When you are in deep freeze, you are experiencing a stress overload. The four major factors which contribute to the excessive demands of overload are: 1) time pressures, 2) excessive responsibility or accountability, 3) lack of support and/or 4) excessive expectations from yourself and those around you. Any one or a combination of these factors can result in damaging stress from overload. Stress overload is evident in the environment, the school, and even the home.[6]

FROZEN AND SPUTTERING

When the body has depleted its energy and the person feels completely exhausted, these things happen: the muscles no longer function as well, or get cramps; the mind doesn't function smoothly; the emotional state is changeable, and one cries or can become hysterical—all signs that the human motor is sputtering and getting ready to stall. Psychological signals that can tell you that your body is reaching the point of stress overload are: difficult decision-making (both major and minor); excessive daydreaming or fantasizing about "getting away from it all;" increased use of cigarettes and alcohol; increased use of tranquilizers and "uppers;" excessive worrying about all things; sudden outbursts of temper and hostility; forgetfulness regarding appointments, deadlines, and dates; thoughts trailing off while speaking or writing. *Does this sound like anyone you know?*[7]

Every pressure in your life that stresses you—charges your bodily systems for action—sets you up for trouble. The trouble lies in how you relate to others and in your bodily system's experience. If you do not effectively deal with your pressure and stress, you and your family will live (or die) in a pile of frustration over your sputtering or stalled engine!

FROZEN TO DEATH

Hans Selye, in his book *Stress Without Distress,* proposes that "stress is the spice of life." He emphasizes that stress is a normal part of living. Too much stress will kill, and freedom from stress will result in death. Stress is part of life and comes from both the positive and the negative. He calls the positive stress *enstress* and the negative stress *distress.*

Enstress is the stress of winning. An achievement, award, victory, exhilaration, promotion, marriage, or birth of a baby are all positive stresses that you want and would not choose to be without. Distress is the stress of losing. Disappointment, loss of job, death of a loved one, divorce, feelings of helplessness and hopelessness, or feelings of inadequacy are all negative stresses that everyone experiences. Since both will destroy you and neither enstress or distress can be avoided, there is only one other option: we must identify our stress and use it rather than be abused by it!

In the 1950's and 1960's at the University of Washington's School of Medicine, Thomas Homes and Richard Rake developed a way of measuring significant life events such as marriage, death, and divorce, along with their impact on people. Each of these events is a significant change in life that may be either positive or negative as a stressor. Holmes and Rake put together a helpful scale to assess your stress levels.

Ongoing studies have shown that an individual who scores 150 or fewer life-change points on the scale in a year is considered in the normal range and is not likely to have been stressed enough to risk illness or injury in subsequent months. Those who scored 150-199 had enough stress so that 37 percent of them had an appreciable health problem. Among people who scored between 200 and 299, 50 percent experienced some sort of illness or injury the following year. Those who had so much crisis in their lives that the score was above 300 were found to have illness or injury in 80 percent of the cases. Of the individuals who scored 350 to 400 points, 90 percent reported significant changes in their health status.[8]

Here's the scale. Test yourself!

Life Event	Value
1. Death of spouse	100
2. Divorce	73
3. Marital separation	65
4. Jail term	63
5. Death of close family member	63
6. Personal injury or illness	53
7. Marriage	50
8. Fired at work	47
9. Marital reconciliation	45
10. Retirement	45
11. Change in health of family member	44
12. Pregnancy	40
13. Sex difficulties	39
14. Gain of new family member	39
15. Business readjustment	39
16. Change in financial state	38
17. Death of close friend	37
18. Change to different line of work	36
19. Change in number of arguments with spouse	35

20.	Mortgage over $40,000	31
21.	Foreclosure of mortgage or loan	30
22.	Change in responsibilities at work	29
23.	Son or daughter leaving home	29
24.	Trouble with in-laws	29
25.	Outstanding personal achievement	28
26.	Spouse begins or stops work	26
27.	Begin or end school	26
28.	Change in living conditions	25
29.	Revision of personal habits	24
30.	Trouble with boss	23
31.	Change in work hours or conditions	20
32.	Change in residence	20
33.	Change in schools	20
34.	Change in recreation	19
35.	Change in church activities	19
36.	Change in social activities	18
37.	Mortgage or loan of less than $40,000	17
38.	Change in number of family get-togethers	15
39.	Change in sleeping habits	15
40.	Change in eating habits	15

The consequences of freezing during the onslaught of the many and varied stresses range from from discomfort to death. One of the simplest and most familiar consequences of stress is the aging process. One of Selye's alternative definitions of stress is "the rate of wear and tear on the body caused by living." Selye seems to consider each human body as having a characteristic amount of total adaptive and coping capability. When this is used up after an accumulated drain of many years, the body is ready to die. In other words, no one dies of old age; everyone eventually dies of stress. It's like being frozen to death![9]

Your body changes through all its systems when encountering a stressor. It's an amazing chain reaction that miraculously prepares every part of your body for survival action. However, as with all charge accounts, *there is a limit!*

CHAPTER 2
Stress Is in the Head

Your mind is the control center of everything that's *you!* It's "the brains of your outfit!" In addition to being a control center, your mind is also a giant tape recorder. It has efficiently recorded everything you've ever said, heard, seen, felt, and done! Through hypnotism a person can be taken all the way back through his life. When he's asked to write his name the way he did at seven, he will print it exactly the way his mind recorded it when he was seven. The operating power of the mind is truly phenomenal!

The mind has also been compared to a computer. What you put into a computer is what comes out, and the same is true for your mind. If you store negative information in your mind, negatives must come out. Garbage in, garbage out!

The mind, which is composed of ten billion billion working parts, has enough storage capacity to accept ten new facts every second. It has been conservatively estimated that the human mind can store an amount of information equivalent to one hundred trillion words, and that none of us uses more than a tiny fraction of this storage space. The mind is a powerful instrument.[1]

The "mental food" you order for your mind will determine the kinds of "psychological digestion" you'll experience. If you order "junk food" for your mind, you may experience "digestion" problems—like "psychological heartburn!"

YOUR OWN STRESS SWITCHBOARDS

Our modern world is an exhilarating place to live. We know more, we can do more, and we possess more than any other society in the history of mankind. Just plug it in, push the buitton, and you have instant everything! But along with having everything is everything happening at such a breathless pace. Everything seems out of control. It's like having your feet firmly planted in midair! The world is passing us by so fast that it becomes nearly impossible for a person to get his/her head together.[2]

But your head is *very together* in that your brain serves as an efficient switchboard in receiving and processing the millions of stressors that flood your life. When your eyes see an angry dog, this message is sent to the brain. Through its switchboard this message is evaluated and an appropriate emotion is selected. The four major options are fear, anger, hunger, and sexual arousal. You'd better hope that nothing goes wrong in this selection when you see that dog; this is no time for hunger or sexual arousal! Based upon the perception and analysis thus far, a decision is required along with an appropriate action. At the same time messages are relayed to the muscular and organic levels which prepare you for that action.

COPPING OUT OR COPING

Your mind sets you up for coping with the problems in this pressure-cooker world. Without coping ability or with a weakened coping ability you gradually move toward cracking up—becoming neurotic or psychotic,

The coping dynamic of your mind has five stages:

perception, analysis, desire, decision, and *action.*

1. *Perception* is the collecting of input through all your senses. These messages are continually being received and stored. Perception is faulty when it is partial or prejudiced. That's why in communication the expression and reception of messages must be as complete as possible.

2. Each perception must be analyzed by checking out your feelings and taking possible action steps. *Analysis* means that you weigh out all possible consequences. What will this cost me? What is the price tag? What will it benefit me? What is the prize? Analysis breaks down when there is little or no time to evaluate your perceptions.

3. *Desire* is the feeling level. This is where you formulate your goals and motivations—your "want to's." Ultimately, people do what they "want to" do! This stage of coping falls apart when people do not articulate clearly what they want.

4. *Decision* is the logical follow-up to desire. In order to cope with or handle a problem well, you must take control. To take control is to choose to make decisions. Too much of life is lived in indecision, which is really a decision in itself. Rather than living life on purpose, most people live by circumstances or by the decisions of others. In my opinion it is at this stage of coping where life can most effectively be handled.

5. *Action* is where the rubber meets the road! Acting out your decisions completes the coping dynamic. The breakdown here is that too many times actions are inhibited. Until appropriate action is taken and fulfilled, coping is incomplete.

Instead of coping with the pressure, most people are copping out. They believe they are escaping by getting away from the pressure, but on the contrary they have embraced the pressure. Coping is the way of processing the pressure with little negative results, but copping out is pressure-cooking the pressure with the results of great psychological and physical damage. If there is no solution (answer, decision, action) when the mind is confronted with a problem or pressure, then the mind essentially sends the problem elsewhere—the stomach, muscles, joints, etc.

THE GROSSEST NATIONAL PRODUCT

Our country's grossest national product is the major substitute for coping ability—drugs. Not just the illegal kind, but all kinds, used in the wrong way.

Despite the great faith and reliance on medicine today (reflected in the 12 percent of the gross national product spent on health care), doctors do not always provide remedies for our ills. And when they don't, we are bitterly disappointed. Given the past successes of medicine—control of infection, diagnostic tools, delicate surgical procedures, chemicals to compensate for our body's deficiencies and difficulties—we have come to expect medicine to solve all our present and future health problems.[3]

So with our unrealistic expectations and demands, we've placed the physician in a difficult position. Less than a quarter of the patients he sees have ailments he can effectively treat. Another 30 to 40 percent of them suffer from long-standing, chronic, degenerative illnesses that are already in such an advanced state of development that all he can offer is palliative treatment to reduce the symptoms or control the pain. Typically, unless the doctor can pinpoint a specific, acute illness, his treatment consists primarily of sympathy and concern plus an assortment of tranquilizers and pain relievers (which account for 25 percent of all medications prescribed).[4]

For the common disorder of simple nervous tension, an alarming number of tranquilizers and barbiturates are prescribed each year. A recent review of tranquilizer use was conducted with 400 pharmacies in the United States. The results indicated that 144 million new prescriptions were written each year for psychotropic drugs, including antidepressants and minor and major tranquilizers. Over half of these prescriptions were for Valium and Librium. If this rate of increase is sustained, according to one psychiatrist, "We can predict that with the arrival of the millennium, in 2000, the whole of America will be taking tranquilizers."[5]

The most widely used drug is alcohol. Seventy-one percent of the United States population drinks at least occasionally, and of these nearly nine million are alcoholics. In her book for the families and employees of problem drinkers, Ruth Maxwell estimates that more than 36 million people in the United States alone (roughly ⅙ of the population) are directly affected by drinking relatives or friends.

When a family member drinks excessively the whole family stability is shaken. There are scenes of drunken behavior accompanied by arguments, promises to reform, denials of the problem, and family attempts to hide the excessive drinking from the outside world.[6]

IT'S ALL IN YOUR HEAD—INITIALLY

To ward off disease or recover health, people normally would rather depend on healers or drugs than to attempt the more difficult task of living wisely. Initially, it's all in your head—to relieve the symptoms or to heal the real problem! This is why, over a century ago, the British physician Sir William Osler told his students, "Ask not what kind of illness the patient has; ask what kind of patient has the illness."

An assumption in traditional approaches to healing is that health or disease are totally dependent upon outside factors, such as bacteria, radiation, crowding, poverty, and all the other factors which have been clearly related to stress and stress-related disorders. There can be no doubt that external issues such as these can in fact predispose individuals toward a state of ill health or can inhibit a person's normal progress of maintaining health and growth, but one of the most important factors to note in the systems designed for stress-alleviation is that the emphasis is now upon internal volition—the mind. It is quite evident that two individuals confronted with virtually the same external circumstances can react quite differently. Individuals can become aware of and create an alternative plan of action to even the most pressing of external circumstances.[7]

Stress is in your head—initially! Then, whether you cope in a healthy way or cop out toward ill health, stress will make its way elsewhere in your system.

CHAPTER 3
The Body Language of Stress

Prehistoric man survived in a dangerous world because, along with an elaborate brain, he possessed the mechanisms for instant physical response when threatened. Picture such a man, thousands of years ago, resting in the sun in front of his cave after the hunt. Suddenly he feels the shadow of a stalking predatory animal. Without thinking he reacts with a mighty rush of automatic resources. He clubs the intruder or fleas into his cave.

Animals respond in the same way today. A snake coils and strikes. A lion springs. A deer runs off into the brush. But when modern men and women feel threatened, various constraints of twentieth-century civilization compel them to clamp a lid on their instinctive impulses. Over the course of time, medical science now tells us, the accumulated effects of these frustrated physical reactions damage the circulatory system, the digestive tract, the lungs, the muscles, and the joints, and they hasten the general process of aging. We don't *catch* migraine, or coronary disease, or perhaps even cancer, despite the virus theory. These sicknesses happen to us because we are rendered vulnerable by the way we choose to live—or, more often, the life that has chosen us.[1]

Stress-induced disorders have long since replaced epidemics of infectious diseases as the major medical problem of the postindustrial nations.[2] As the pressure seeds of problems and disease blow about our world, mankind has become fertile ground for these destructive seeds to grow and mature. That fertile ground basically consists of what goes into the mouth, what does not come out of the mouth, and lack of bodily movement.

UNABLE TO STOP SWALLOWING

The difference between feeling up or down, sane or insane, calm or freaked out, inspired or depressed depends in large measure upon what we put into our mouths. In many respects we are digging our graves with out teeth!

There is an appropriate saying that "The stomach expands to accommodate the amount of junk food available!" One of the most deadly, disease-ridden junk food is refined sugar. Sugar addiction is a worldwide phenomenon today. It is not uncommon in counseling to discover that much of the deviant behavior in an individual is due to sugar addiction.

Modern Americans consume 2½ pounds of processed sugar per person per week. This accounts for about 25 percent of all calories—and these are totally lacking in the vitamins and minerals needed to metabolize sugar. Furthermore, the sugar is rapidly absorbed, leading to overstimulation of insulin and eventually to exhaustion of the pancreas. By contrast, Westerners 150 years ago ate only about two pounds of sugar per year—7.5 times less.[3]

After years of sugar days, the end result is damaged adrenals. They are worn out not from overwork but from continual whiplash. Overall production of hormones is low, and amounts don't dovetail. This disturbed function, out of balance, is reflected all around the endocrine circuit. The brain may soon have trouble telling the real from the unreal; we're likely to go off half-cocked. When stress comes our way, we go to pieces because we no longer have a healthy endocrine system to cope with it. Day-to-day efficiency lags, we're always tired, and we never seem to get anything done. It's the sugar blues![4]

In addition to the stress effects of sugar, there is another food stressor which has become a way of life—caffeine. According to John T. Greden, a University of Michigan psychiatrist, excessive caffeine intake from coffee breaks and soft drinks can induce behavior disturbances. Symptoms of excessive caffeine are nervousness, insomnia, headache, sweaty palms, and perhaps ulcers. All that is required to produce such severe reactions is approximately 250 mg. of caffeine (one cup of coffee contains 100-150 mg., one cup of tea about 65-75 mg.). Based on clinical observations, Greden indicates that excessive amounts of caffeine can lead to circulatory failure, nausea, vomiting, diarrhea, stomach pains, and even occasionally a peptic ulcer.[5]

Many "foods" become stressors to our bodies and will be discussed later.

UNABLE TO SPIT IT OUT

Another stressor to the body is being unable to articulate strong feelings—unable to spit it out. These feelings could be fear, anger, guilt, etc. Pat Allen, a popular counselor and seminarist, says, "If your mouth won't say it, your body will!" This kind of sentence is one of the producers of the body language of stress!

Fear of confronting the real problem encourages

this stressful silence. An individual is confronted with a stressful situation which is extremely difficult for him or her to resolve. This situation becomes overwhelming, and he sees no relief from it. As a result, he makes an unconscious choice which allows him a means of coping with this irresolvable situation. One means of resolution is to develop a psychosomatic disorder, such as a migraine headache, which affects him so severely that he is incapacitated and released from the responsibilities which weigh so heavily upon him. This symptom frees him from the necessity of dealing with the more complex and unmanageable stress situation. Now he is ill, and his peers and family modify their expectations and demands accordingly. His illness postpones or even prevents a confrontation with his real, underlying problem.[6]

UNABLE TO MOVE

The last and most universal ingredient to the fertile ground in which pressure seeds grow and blossom is the lack of action. When pressured, the body stresses for *action*. This is part of the excess baggage of civilization.

Certain stressor foods, the lack of communication of strong feelings, and the general lack of activity prepare the body to talk for itself through damaging stress. It's the body language of stress making noise throughout the body's systems.

THE CARDIOVASCULAR SYSTEM
Heart Attack

Each year more deaths in the United States are attributed to diseases of the cardiovascular system than to any other kind of death. Coronary disease has increased fivefold in the United States in the last 50 years. Something in the nature of contemporary lifestyles and social organization appears to be responsible. The total cost of heart disease to the United States has been estimated at more than 30 billion dollars per year.[7]

More and more it is beginning to appear that the single greatest cause of heart attack is the stress of life. This view has been held with special enthusiasm by two San Francisco cardiologists named Meyer Friedman and Ray Rosenman. These men divide the population into two broad categories, Type A and Type B. The Type A person is ambitious, aggressive, self-demanding, competitive, and pushing to be successful. He or she "goes all the time" and is driven by the clock. In contrast, Type B people are more casual. They are less competitive, less worried about time, and not so preoccupied with achievement. The two types even differ in their approach to relaxation. Type B can enjoy casual conversation and forget his work during a game of golf. Type A competes as intensely in sports as elsewhere. After studying this problem for over 20 years, Drs. Friedman and Rosenman believe that when people live a Type A lifestyle there is a seven-times-higher risk of heart attack than with a Type B mode of living.[8]

Most studies repeatedly demonstrate that stress and behavior are principal culprits in the high incidence of heart attacks among middle-aged Americans. They also show that personality patterns play a vital role as well, and that both stress and personality patterns can be changed before it is too late.[9]

An extremely interesting study evaluated the difference between 64 heart patients and 109 normal people. It was discovered from their descriptions of themselves and their life situations that they differed in three primary ways: 1) excessive overtime work; 2) hostility toward others who slowed them down; and 3) dissatisfaction with their jobs. As you can see, your stressed body speaks for itself![10]

Hypertension

Hypertension, or high blood pressure, is one of the most insidious medical problems of our time. By conservative estimates, it affects approximately 15 percent of the adult population of the United States. High blood pressure is listed as the primary cause of 60,000 deaths per year. There has been an alarming increase in the incidence of high blood pressure among teenagers and young people in the last few years. Probably fewer than one-eighth of all hypertensives in the United States are being treated effectively.[11]

The typical hypertensive is just as ambitious as the heart-attack type, but a great deal less self-confident. He spends his life in unspoken conflict with authority. But, unlike the heart-attack type, he has little expectation of winning that conflict, with the result that he may imprison himself in a job that is beneath his capacity, with little responsibility and little future. His life is filled with a sense of drudgery, slavery, and hopeless labor.

In childhood he most often got along poorly with his father and was not allowed to talk back, so that a mixture of *anger* and *guilt* have been building up inside him for many years, to be directed in adulthood against his employer, or, in the case of some husbands and wives, against each other.

Hypertensives' relationships with their mothers were close. They never seem to break away, and their lives swing back and forth between longing to be taken care of and resentment against overprotection. Hypertensives are easily upset—by criticism, by disorder, by imperfection of any kind—but are unable to handle upsetting situations.[12]

Migraine

Headaches cause more than half the visits to doctors' offices in this country. Migraine strikes one in eight Americans at some point in their lives, and is caused by dilation of the blood vessels in the scalp.

As for the coronary type, the meaning of life is work. The average migraine patient cannot handle leisure. Basically he is insecure. What he really wants is to be loved, but he will settle for being admired or simply approved of—anything to still his gnawing sense of worthlessness. It is for this reason that he drives himself so hard, selflessly taking on thankless chores and burdening himself with ever-increasing responsibilities. He is conscientious, rigid, even fanatical.

The emotional tension of the migraine all builds to a strike-point—when he is forced to leisure! All the feelings he buried away are now bringing on the pain![13]

THE DIGESTIVE SYSTEM
Ulcers

When you are under pressure, the body's clearest signal of that fact may come when you swallow. The effects turn up in the esophagus, the stomach, the duodenum, the small intestine, the colon, the rectum, and all the links in between. Other organs involved in the processing of food, such as the kidneys and pancreas, are also victims of stress.

More than eight million Americans suffer from ulcers. People with stomach ulcers have gastric systems that are in constant motion or constant emotion. Their tendencies are to be go-getters who desire for themselves independence from the rest of the world or for success. The ulcer type is full of hostility but will not express it because of his great desire to be loved. He constantly lives with an unexpressed inner rage.

Ulcerative Colitis

In ulcerative colitis, the membrane of the colon so deteriorates that it bleeds a great deal and may eventually perforate. Pressure from the job or family, or long-repressed pressure in childhood, make the colon vulnerable to the damage from the inevitable onslaught of daily stress.

These patients are usually very tidy, restrained people, notably mild and mannerly, conscientious, punctual, and inhibited in the normal patterns of their lives. They are also unusually thin-skinned, alert to real or imagined insults from the world. One of their greatest fears is rejection, and they express all their despair through their gastrointestinal equipment![14]

THE IMMUNOLOGICAL SYSTEM
Infections

Run-down people get infections easily, and stress runs peole down. It is now known that stress actually disturbs the immunological system itself. In the words of Hans Selye, "If a microbe is in or around us all the time and yet causes no disease until we are exposed to stress, what is the 'cause' of our illness, the microbe or the stress?''

When a person is in good health it sometimes seems that the human body is a fortress against infection, with a capable crew of tireless guards—known in immunology as antibodies—on patrol night and day, keeping the interior clear of the enemy. But it is not that way at all. Actually, we are indwelt by microbial agents just as thickly as feudal lords were surrounded by serfs, with many of the vassals living in the castle 24 hours a day. When the lord's control begins to slip, the vassals may suddenly turn on him and take over.

The body's defenses against invasion do not operate at full force at all times. In the first months of life the immunity system is still under construction, and in old age it begins to deteriorate: both babies and the elderly are very susceptible to infection. And so are people under stress. Stress weakens the immune response greatly!

What happens is that emotional problems stir up the hypothalamus in the brain. The hypothalamus is the immune center in the body which builds up the body's antibodies for fighting off disease. The hypothalamus then stirs up the pituitary gland, which in turn stirs up the adrenal glands. And the adrenals start sending out increased amounts of a kind of hormone called glucocorticoid. It's these excess glucocorticoids that do the damage. Under their influence a person produces fewer antibodies, and his inflammatory response dwindles.[15]

Allergies and Arthritis
People get sick not only when their resistance

lowers, but also when it rises too high! These are the people with the inflammatory diseases like an allergy or arthritis—diseases in which the body is injured not by some alien microbe but by its *own* protective devices, senselessly firing away at a harmless challenge, and sometimes at no challenge at all.[16]

There seems to be no outside invader in rheumatoid arthritis, yet doctors keep searching for this proposed phantom. When the body's immune system becomes confused and aimlessly fires away, allergies occur, attacking the digestive tract, the nose, the lungs, and the skin. But with arthritis the immune system is so confused that the body's defense system does not aimlessly fire but fires with aim at its own body! This is known as autoimmunity. Here the immune system fails in its most important task—the distinction between self and non-self. It then manufactures antibodies against the person's own tissues. So now the body's own immune system is actually attacking itself!

Cancer

In cancer, the body also fails in its task of surveillance—the task of recognizing an enemy within its gates—but with reverse results. Here foe is mistaken for friend, and a deadly enemy is allowed to live and multiply inside the body without interference. Cancerous mutations are apparently a regular occurrence in the lives of perfectly healthy people, who never know it because their immune systems destroy the mutant cell before it can multiply.[17]

Many things can cause mutations—chemicals, burns, injuries, X-rays, viruses, etc. When a mutation is allowed to grow like a "friend" in the body, the immune system has obviously been confused and weakened. What is it that deceives and weakens the immune defenses? *Stress!*

Drs. Leshan and Worthington, studying hundreds of cancer patients, reported that 72 percent of these patients had experienced the loss of an important relationship within two years prior to the tumor diagnosis. Many of these patients (47 percent) had difficulty expressing hostile feelings toward people, and 37 percent still experienced tension over the death of a parent, which often had occurred many years earlier. Over and over again, the recent lives of cancer patients were linked to loss and life change.[18]

A profile of the cancer victim has been derived from psychological testing of people of various ages and diagnostic categories. Typically, a cancer patient has suffered severe emotional disturbance in early childhood, up to the age of 15. Most frequently this resulted from his/her relationships with parents or a breakup in the unity of the family. Because of divorce, the death of either parent, chronic friction between the parents, or prolonged separation of one or both parents from the child, the child experienced a great sense of loss, loneliness, anxiety, and rejection. He felt he had failed in his earliest attempts to form warm and satisfying relationships. His reaction to this may have been to overcompensate by trying constantly to please others and to win their affection. If he continued to be frustrated in these attempts, his anger, loneliness, hopelessness, and self-hatred become more pronounced, with anxiety and depression becoming his constant companions.

Later in life, cancer victims are frequently described by their friends as exceptionally fine, thoughtful, gentle, uncomplaining people, and "almost too good to be true."

All of these traits appear to be an amplification of the frustrated need to win love and affection. Underneath, feelings of hostility are bottled up and suppressed rather than brought to the surface and worked through. This "too-good-to-be-true" trait can assume an almost martyrlike quality, and many cancer researchers believe that it masks a chronic, low-key depression.

During adulthood, a cancer victim usually achieves love, healthy relationships, and some measure of success through marriage, a career, or parenthood. For the first time in his life he may feel genuinely happy and optimistic. However, since this happiness depends upon external factors—spouse, children, and job—it is inevitable that the emotional matrix which supports the individual will change. Change may take the form of death of a mate, loss of a job, retirement, or children leaving the home to embark on their own lives. With a high degree of predictability, such individuals are found to succumb to cancer within six months to a year. When the disease is discovered, their despair deepens, and the classic "helpless-hopeless" cycle is initiated.[19]

And what seems to be the major contributing factor to the breakdown of the immune system? Not *just* stress, but *family stress!*

THE SKELETAL-MUSCULAR SYSTEM
Aches and Pains
One of the clearest languages of the body is com-

municated through the skeletal-muscular system, from a simple frown or smile of the face to the aches and pains of the muscles.

When a person feels like acting but does not allow himself to act, his muscles remain tensed in readiness, sometimes for months or years at a time, immobilized into a state of tightness even during sleep. The repression of action will most normally produce a variety of aches, pains, and spasms.[20]

Arthritis

The most crucial piece of machinery relative to the muscles and bones is the joint. In addition to the breakdown of the immune system (which inflames the joints, causing arthritis), there seems to be another contributing factor. When the brain sends forth its massive doses of adrenaline throughout the body in preparation for action, the body is filled with energy fluids. The body is ready—ready for some kind of exertion! If that exertion isn't made, then the energy fluids remain ready but useless, and they attack primarily the joints, which causes inflammation. This is when a person literally begins "stewing in his own juices"!

Much of the repression of action with the arthritic is due to the repression of anger and hostility. In most studies the rheumatoid arthritic was found to be somewhat shy socially, worried, and unable to express anger easily. Since such people find it difficult to communicate or act out their feelings, the skeletal-muscular system will speak a language of its own—*pain and injury!*

The body language of stress is very articulate. What is your body saying to you?

CHAPTER 4
People Pressure

Who needs people? They bruise, abuse, and use you! The competition conflicts, and confusion within relationships is enough to do you in! Just think—without people we could eliminate most of our pressure—*people pressure.*

People bruise people! Nearly half of all marriages end in divorce. Over 40 percent of all children born in this decade will spend part of their youth in single-parent homes. Only 16 percent of today's families fit the traditional concept of family— father, mother, and children, with dad the breadwinner and mom at home to care for the family. The fractured family bruises everyone in the family; no one escapes the damaging effect. Rejection in relationships is the big bruiser for both broken families and the unbroken (but slightly cracked) families. Men are rejected for their seemingly unfeeling, dictatorial approach to relationship or for their unmanly, indecisive leadership style. Women are rejected for their nagging, critical approach to relationships or for their weak, clinging-vine style of hanging on to relationships. Children are rejected either for being children or for attempting to act like adults. Parents are rejected for not understanding their children. People are rejected for success and failure, for caring too much and caring too little, for running off at the mouth and for not moving the mouth at all, for everything people-types do and don't do!

People are bruisers when relationships are

severed or broken in any way. Research supports the view that loss of an individual's place in the community is related to illness. One study discovered that voluntary exclusion or forced expulsion from a community or group coincided, *with astonishing frequency,* with the onset or the relapse of a peptic ulcer. That's a bruiser![1]

THE ABUSERS
People pressure also comes through the abusers. Physical abuse of women and children has become a frightening act within the family, with epidemic proportions. What is even more disheartening is what counselors are discovering everywhere: that physical abuse, including beatings and molestation, is being uncovered as a major contributing factor in the psychological and physical problems of multitudes of adults. People everywhere have been scarred deeply by abusers in their past.

Unfortunately, the very people who are to be lifting us up are the same people who are throwing us down—literally. Most physical abuse occurs within the family *by* family members. With all of this abusive activity within the home, is it any real surprise that 54 percent of all murders are within the family?

THE USERS
Instead of loving people and using things, society's motto today is to love things and use people! The users become experts in the surfacey relationships. In-depth, intimate, and meaningful relationships are foreign. Therefore, the people-users are using people more and enjoying it less. The users become victims of their own philosophy of

relationships. They too feel used!

People-users are career people rather than people with a career. They have effectively married their businesses. Because of this unnatural "marriage," people don't spend much time together anymore. There are at least 700,000 computer couples who, because of jobs in differing cities, spend only "part-time" together. Part-time relationships create part-time people—people with pressure!

People-users also have an optical problem—the big "I"! Daniel Yankelovich, a prominent sociological researcher, declared in his book *New Rules:* "Among the people I interviewed, many truly committed self-fulfillment seekers focus so sharply on their own needs that instead of achieving the more intimate relationships they desire, they grow farther apart from others. In dwelling on their own needs, they discover that the inner journey brings loneliness and depression. They are caught in a debilitating contradiction: their goal is to expand their lives by reaching beyond the self, but the strategy they employ constricts them, drawing them inward toward an ever-narrowing, closed-off "I". People want to enlarge their choices but, seeking to 'keep all options open,' they diminish them."

The bruisers, abusers, and users pour on the pressure. All three are helping to blow the family apart.

SUICIDE IN SLOW MOTION

James Lynch's book on the subject of loneliness demonstrates how stressful loneliness (the failure of relationships) can be. Lynch noted that for major causes of death in this country (heart disease, cancer, and automobile accidents), death rates were higher among single, widowed, and divorced individuals (for all races and both sexes) than for married individuals. In the United States, unmarried men between the ages of 45 and 54 have a 123 percent greater death rate than married men. Lynch concluded that "in a number of cases of premature coronary disease and premature death, interpersonal unhappiness, the lack of love, and human loneliness seem to appear as the root causes of the physical problems." These suggestions are further underscored by the fact that the health status of married people seems to be improving, while the health of unmarried people is not.[2]

Our society, suffocated with loneliness and failure, is more concerned with the relief of pain and suffering than at any previous time. One-quarter of all medical prescriptions are for tranquilizers or pain-relieving drugs. More than half of the people who see physicians do so for nonspecific complaints rather than for definite physical ailments. Our newspapers are full of advertisements urging lonely people, who may be despondent with the pain of loneliness, to call a Help Line or Hot Line. If you cannot find love, you can call a dating service and a computer will match you to another lonely person. If your loneliness and irresponsibility fall into one of several common patterns, you may join an old, established group, such as Alcoholics Anonymous or a new group, such as Recovery Incorporated, Gamblers Anonymous, or Neurotics Anonymous. All of these groups bring lonely people together to relieve their suffering (caused through loneliness and failure) by getting them to help one another become more responsible through mutual involvement.[3]

The need for involvement has been built into our nervous systems, and we always feel pain when we have no involvement. The pain warns us to seek involvement with others. If we fail in the attempt, there is always one possibility left for involvement: *ourselves*. Unsatisfactory and painful as this is in comparison with involvement with others who are worthwhile, involvement with ourselves will reduce and sometimes eliminate temporarily the pain of being alone. But because we need involvement with others, self-involvement is an inadequate alternative; we cannot fool our nervous system for long. Quickly dissatisfied with our self-involvement, it again responds with pain and we respond with further self-deception in response to the pain.[4]

To avoid the fact that we are really involved with ourselves, we have learned to focus our attention on a creation outside ourselves. We create and concentrate on an idea, such as an obsessive fear of germs; a behavior, such as compulsive gambling; a physical symptom, such as a migraine headache; or an emotion, such as depression. We focus on these self-creations as if they were real and separate from us. Keeping overly clean, gambling, suffering with (and treating) a headache, or being depressed then becomes our problem in place of our true problem—loneliness. Loneliness is the lack of relationship or the lack of a healthy relationship. We have *chosen* to act as we do because we desperately hope that the symptom or the behavior will provide enough involvement to satisfy what we should get from other people. Over thousands of years of loneliness, we humans have developed numerous self-involved symptoms and behaviors to keep us company and to reduce our pain of loneliness.[5]

Most medical practice is based on relieving pain. Today millions of people go to doctors in an attempt to relieve the pain of depression and its close relatives—a host of nagging, painful complaints such as fatigue, headache, intestinal upset, muscular aches, and loss of interest in sex. Many doctors, however, do not understand that depression and most other such symptoms and complaints are companions. Trained to rid people of pain, they respond to the complaints of lonely and failing people by prescribing drugs that treat the aching symptom and not the true source of the problem—loneliness. It's placing a Band-Aid on a hemorrhage! Lonely people are running themselves into the ground. It's suicide in slow motion.[6]

THE CHANGE OF LIFE

Life is filled with changes, and those changes wear and tear away at people. Change is the constant and unrelenting undertow which induces stress in people at levels that threaten their health and well-being. The period from 1900 until the present stands apart from every other period in human history as a time of incredible change. One consequence of the bewildering variety of changes taking place within this century has been a complete metamorphosis in the typical American lifestyle.[7]

This age of change is truly the age of stress! There are two primary factors which contribute to the age of stress: *space for people* and *the pace of people*.

SPACE FOR PEOPLE

In 1900 most Americans lived on farms or in rural

areas. Only 40 percent of them lived in urban areas. However, with the rapid development of technology, transportation, and big corporations, as well as the concentration of large manufacturing operations in the cities, a steady migration brought most Americans to the cities. By 1975 about 75 percent of Americans lived in urban areas. And of the remaining rural 25 percent, only about 4 percent could be classified as farmers. Most of them still worked in cities even though living rurally. This has revolutionized the style of living for a large fraction of the American population, making them much less self-sufficient and much more dependent on the logistic systems that serve the cities.[8]

It's a struggle for space because of the crowded conditions. The city-dweller usually eats, sleeps, and lives within a few yards of other people whom he knows only casually. He drives to work on a crowded freeway or street, works in a crowded building, rides crowded elevators, eats lunch in a crowded restaurant, and stands in crowded lines.

Although people vary in their tolerance and appetite for contact with other humans, every person has a comfort level that can be exceeded. Having even one person within your "space" (within 3 to 5 feet) will make you somewhat more aroused than simply being alone. As a creature, you react in a very basic biological way to the presence of others in your spatial world. Prolonged close contact without means for retreat and relaxation can be extremely stressful for most people.[9]

We are not only crowded, but we are connected to one another worldwide. Interconnectedness has probably done more to change the lives, beliefs, values, aspirations, and habits of Americans than any other single thing. And it has probably led to a greater share of the increasing stress load than any other factor. With TV, radio, nationwide newspapers and magazines, and the extremely efficient telephone, Americans have come to conceive of themselves as interlocked with one another and interlocked with all other countries of the world.[10]

Dr. Karl Albrecht, organization development consultant, says: "It is my opinion that the high-speed communication media within which we live have the effect of overloading us with information about problems beyond our control, of alarming us with incidents far removed from our immediate experience, and of helping us to worry vaguely and without focus. This is an extremely important component of the twentieth-century stress diet experienced by the typical American.[11]

THE PACE OF PEOPLE

The space is crowded and closely connected, but the pace of people fuels the interconnected crowds. Living in the presence of large numbers of people induces a relatively high level of alertness in the city-dweller. Everyday activities such as sprinting across the street to avoid oncoming traffic, or jamming on the brakes to avoid a spurting pedestrian, require the city-dweller to stay alert and act quickly.[12]

Mobility adds to the pace of people. Americans change jobs on the average of three to five years. To look at it another way, over 20 percent of all families in America move each year. The magnitude of moving 36 million Americans from city to city is the same as if the combined populations of Cambodia, Ghana, Guatemala, Honduras, Iraq,

Israel, Mongolia, Nicaragua, and Tunisia were forced from their homes and relocated. That news would make front-page headlines, but the huge migration within America seems to go on without much flourish.[13]

The primary form of anxiety from the great mobility of lifestyle is the loss of a sense of permanence. This loss relates to another facet of the pace of people—consumerism. Americans buy almost any product that appears on the market provided it is well-packaged and has sufficient advertising exposure—from microwave ovens to CB radios to Pet Rocks. It's almost a disease of preoccupation with things—things that are *new* and things that you must have *now.* And when it breaks or gets old, throw it away!

The apparent effect of this compulsive consuming and of the transient nature of the things acquired has been to create in the back of the American mind a general impression that nothing lasts—or even should last. This feeling of instability penetrates everything, including relationships. The thinking is, "Maybe relationships don't last or were never meant to." Therefore, throw it away![14]

Another facet of the pace of people is the great shift from a society that is physically active to a sedentary lifestyle. Most Americans do not have to work hard physically anymore. For example, over half the work force produces, processes, and handles information. Because of all of our conveniences (plus TV) we are raising generation after generation of children who are almost as sedentary and out-of-condition as their parents. It is very likely that a sedentary child will carry this habit pattern into his adult years, living in a style that promotes poor health, low vitality, overweight, and susceptibility to such major diseases as heart attack, stroke, and other degenerative disorders.[15]

LOOSE LIVERS AND LIVING LOOSELY

The most dramatic illustration of people pressure and its consequences is found within the health statistics of Utah and Nevada. In Utah, the population is 72 percent Mormon. Mormonism is a religion with strong family ties and community obligations. Nevada's chief industry is gambling, and its population includes many rootless, isolated, mobile people. Of all the 50 states, Utah has the lowest incidence of tuberculosis, major cardiovascular diseases, psychological illnesses, hypertension, infectious diseases, and infant mortality. It ranks 49th in flu, pneumonia, and arteriosclerosis. But in neighboring Nevada, the health patterns are dramatically different. It is at or near the top of the list in most of these same ailments. While Utah's nonurbanized lifestyle may partially account for the population's health, the social cohesion and community stability of the Mormons surely support their well-being.[16]

People pressure! We are caught in a difficult dilemma because of people. We can't live with them and we can't live without them. People can support you or stress you. As you will see later in this book, it's all up to you!

CHAPTER 5
Little People Under Pressure

Most of us think of stress as an adult phenomenon. But today's pressures to cope, to succeed, and to win are every bit as taxing—indeed, as dangerous—for children as they are for adults. Unlike the children of the previous generation who were raised under less discipline, the children of the eighties are the hurried children: forced to achieve more, earlier, than any other generation; outfitted in designer jeans and a whole array of adult costumes; faced with divorce and single-parent families. Their traditional rites of passage come too early; their fears of failure are constant.

From every corner of society our children are faced with forced blooming: if a child doesn't read by the age of four we label him or her a failure; television and the movies tell our young teens that sex is in and childhood is out; and parents increasingly look to a child to rescue them from their despair brought on by divorce, role conflict and job dissatisfaction. These pressures and others are overwhelming our children.*

MOST PRESSURED VOCATION—PARENTING

Girl meets boy. They "fall in love" and marry. One becomes larger than the other (normally the girl) and they have a baby. Now both girl and boy

*I strongly recommend Dr. David Elkind's book *The Hurried Child* as additional resource on children under stress. This outstanding pioneer book offers a fresh look at children growing up too fast too soon.

are promoted to the most important and pressurized position on earth—parents!

Parenting is the responsibility of growing people. As parents in the people-growing business we are bombarded by four pressures.

First, *we as parents are extremely confused.* One group of psychologists tells us not to spank children or we'll damage their psyche. Another equally educated group of psychologists explains that we must spank children so that we are able to mold their psyche. So that leaves the average parent in a paralyzed state of confusion. What does the confused parent do? Sometimes the parent spanks and sometimes he doesn't spank—all for the same crime!

We are also confused about whether our children are children or just miniature adults. We harass our children with some of the emotional-intellectual-social demands of adulthood but at the same time treat them—often ostentatiously—as mere children. Sometimes we go so far as to infantilize them (even adolescents) by permitting them to have messy rooms, to leave things lying around, to get up at odd hours, and to eat junk food. We recognize children's special estate at the very same time that we hurry them to grow up too fast.[1]

Second, *we as parents are afraid.* The threat of violence, robbery, vehicle accidents, and peer pressure of drugs and alcohol is increasingly a real possibility for us and our children. There is a floating fear that no matter what we do as parents, we still may lose our children to injury or death.

There is also the fear of being extremely incompetent as a parent. We have been conned into believing that only the "experts"—doctors, psychologists, clergy—know the best thing to do as parents for our children. Therefore, since we fear our incompetence so greatly, we act fearfully incompetent!

Third, *we as parents are alone.* In previous generations our parents and grandparents had lots of help in parenting their children. My parents had the help of six other families—my aunts and uncles. All of these relatives lived within a 35-mile radius of our home. Today families are scattered throughout the United States, if not the world. Most of us parents are left all alone to grow our little people.

In addition to being alone in parenting, without the support of relatives, more and more parents are experiencing an even greater aloneness—single-parenting. Nearly one in five families with children are now headed by one parent, an increase of 70 percent since 1970. In 1979, 17 percent of all one-parent families with children were maintained by the mother alone and 2 percent by the father alone. The panic of being a single parent with all its overcompensations is worse than the problem. But the whole scene is not good.[2]

Fourth, *we as parents are professionally insecure.* The stressors of technological unemployment, inflation, recession, and high interest rates place parents in a stressfully insecure situation.

This insecurity has become one of the most pivotal problems in parenting, because it has turned parents into self-centered people. Selfishness and parenting do not compliment each other; they are mutually exclusive.

The prevalence of self-centeredness puts us squarely in a dilemma in regard to raising children. If it is to be done well, child-rearing requires, more than most activities of life, a good deal of decentering from one's own needs and perspectives. Such decentering is relatively easy when a society is stable and when there is an extended, supportive structure that the parent can depend upon. When the parent is busy surviving, the people-growing process suffers.[3]

HOMOGENIZED PEOPLE

Just as parents are pressured, so the children are under pressure. As a matter of fact, kids are being placed in the *adult* pressure-cooker—a pot only meant for adults. No matter how unfair this seems to be, there is a massive movement toward thrusting children prematurely into adulthood. It's a homogenization process of mixing adults and children into the same mold. Homogenizing children into adulthood creates a stress overload!

INFORMATION OVERLOAD

A common family member within every American family is TV. Brother TV gets more attention than any other member of the family and gives more input than anyone else. The average child has viewed 13,000 violent deaths before getting out of high school. He has also viewed 20,000 commercials![4]

BROTHER TV

Brother TV is at times the family baby-sitter, but almost always robs children of their childhood. TV communicates the same information to everyone simultaneously, regardless of age, sex, level of education, or life experience. Therefore TV eliminates many of the important ways that we distinguish between children and adults. For example, one of the main differences between an adult and a child is that the adult knows about certain facets of life—its mysteries, its contradictions, its violence, its tragedies—that are not considered suitable for children to know, or even accessible to children.[5]

What TV does is to bring the whole culture out of the closet, because programs need a constant supply of fascinating information. In its quest for new and sensational ventures to hold its audience, TV must tap every existing taboo in the culture: homosexuality, incest, divorce, promiscuity, corruption, adultery, and terrible displays of violence and sadism. As a consequence, these become as familiar to the young as they do to adults. The new media tend to obliterate classes of people, particularly the difference between what we call adulthood and childhood.[6]

Neil Postman, Professor of Communication Arts and Sciences at New York University, offers some examples of homogenization: "Some of the highest-paid models in America are now 12- and 13-year-old girls who are presented to us in the guise of sexually enticing adults, so much so that old-timers might yearn for the innocence of Lolita compared to these. If you look at the children as they are depicted on situation comedies, such as "Love Boat" or "Different Strokes," you find that they're really little adults. Their language is the same as adults, their interests are the same, their sexuality is the same. It's getting harder to find children who are portrayed as children in many prime-time shows.

"In one hand-lotion commercial, viewers are

shown a mother and daughter and challenged to tell which is which. To me, this tells us that it is considered desirable that a mother should not look older than her daughter, or that a daughter should not look younger than her mother. In that there is no clear concept of what is means to be an adult, there can be no concept of what is means to be a child."[7]

One result of TV's homogenization of adulthood and childhood is that it begins to show up in other facets of society. The language of adults and children tends to merge into the same content, as well as their interests, dress, sports, and amusements. For example, there are fewer and fewer characteristics in children's clothing or, for that matter, in children's games. Things like Little League Baseball or Pee Wee Football are modeled after televised sports in their organization and emotional style. Now you need sophisticated equipment, verbal umpires, and emotionally upset spectators. And kids don't play so much for pleasure as they do to enhance their reputation or keep their parents satiated.[8]

The TV "family" time slot is really a farce, because neither children nor the TV is turned off at the shift from the family hour to adults only. In fact, between midnight and two in the morning there are something like 750,000 children throughout America watching television every day! Some people have a fantasy that after 10 P.M. children are not watching television; that's nonsense![9]

In addition to Brother TV, information overload includes books, magazines, movies, and records. Children's reading material is coming into a new realism. This is good in one sense, in that previously kids' literature was filled with a childhood innocence that actually never existed. With the new realism kids are exposed to the way life really is!

However, even though the new realism is for real and helps to prepare children for the real world, this approach pours on the pressure to hurry up the child to grow up too fast. Much of the new realism in the literature for young children hurries them in two ways. The task of self-discovery is more difficult when children are presented with the problems and difficulties of other people before they have had a chance to find meaning in their own lives. Because many children are never exposed to material like fairly tales, they are deprived of a literature that would help them make sense and give order to their experience. A basic maxim of mental health, recognized long before there was anything like psychoanalysis, is that you have to be able to help yourself before you can help others.[10]

Ratings Aren't for Kids

Like TV and books, the movies have moved toward a new realism in topics, in language, and in characterization as parents have become more relaxed about watching it. With the advent of cable television in both homes and hotels, unsupervised children have access to sexually explicit and violent films. Film ratings, like PG, R, and X, are ambiguous at best, and no one seems to take them too seriously. The theater ratings seem almost ridiculous, since X-rated films are available to children at home on late-night cable television. Ratings are only another way of marketing.[11]

Humming: The Way Out

Dr. Elkind (*The Hurried Child*) says concerning the information overload of the record business: "Clearly, the most underestimated influence on young people today is the record business. Perhaps because most adults find the level of sound obnoxious, the harmonics jarring, and the lyrics incomprehensible, we prefer to ignore the impact of rock music on our offspring. As a culture, we are visually oriented, and this is why we are so concerned about the sex and violence presented on television and in films. But music can influence young people as much as any visual media.

"Music promoted for the youth market (the primary market) is directed not so much to the conscious as to the unconscious or subliminal level of awareness and thus is too easily dismissed. Perhaps more importantly, music directed at young people is aimed not so much at hurrying them into adulthood as at providing escapes from the pressures to grow up fast."[12]

No Work/No Play Equals Dullness

The most significant effect of information overload is that children are left in an inactive and sedentary state. The precise thing needed for the relief of stress is action. But information overload freezes children in inactivity and boredom.

Boredom appears to prey quite heavily upon American adolescents. Some psychologists suggest that as many as 20 percent of American adolescents are psychologically handicapped by boredom and depression. Such a handicap may lead to loss of self-esteem and eventually to self-destructive behaviors such as drug abuse and even suicide. The fact that suicide has risen to be one of the leading causes of adolescent death appears to support this contention. As a result, billions of dollars are spent each year on specialized entertainment and diversions for adolescents. All of these signs appear to indicate that, through massive technological advances, we are literally boring many Americans to death, especially our children. Pac-Man fever is only one of the many diseases with the side effects of boredom and dullness![13]

RESPONSIBILITY OVERLOAD

According to current estimates, there may be two to four million latchkey kids (kids at home alone caring for themselves) between the ages of seven and thirteen. This latchkey experience moves the child into parental, adult responsibilities.

An interesting example of the latchkey scene was reported in *Newsweek:* ''When they persuaded their divorced father to take them out of the day-care center last year and let them fend for themselves, the three Bradley sisters become the envy of all their friends. 'It's more fun than being cooped up,' says 12-year-old Ann. Now, after doing their chores, the trio can bike and tree-climb to their heart's delight in the cul-de-sac outside their home in suburban Houston. 'I come home and the kitchen is clean for me to make dinner, and everyone is happy,' beams their dad, oil company executive Gerald Bradley! 'I sometimes worry they might be losing a little of their childhood too quickly, but they seem to enjoy the responsibility.' '' This worry is well-founded because of the stress experienced from this premature thrust into adulthood!

''Though the latchkey experience may well produce more self-reliant adults, the kids have mixed feelings about it. 'I know I'll be prepared when I grow up,' says Gilliam, a Sonoma, California 11-year-old who takes care of her younger brothers as well as herself while her single mother is at work. Nearby in San Francisco, 13-year-old Chris copes reasonably smoothly with domestic life, except for the overloaded dishwasher or underdone chicken. His ambitions are clear-cut: to marry a woman like his grandmother, who 'cooks and even irons sheets.' "[14]

There is nothing wrong with responsibility. It's the overload that causes the damage. That overload level is when a child is forced into adult responsibilities before sorting through his or her childhood development.

EMOTIONAL OVERLOAD

Information and responsibility overloads have a major effect—emotional overload! When you realize that over a fifth of all violent crimes are committed by youths under 18, that one million children are living on the streets, with ⅓ of them supporting themselves as prostitutes, and that alcohol and drug abuse are rising sharply, then you can begin to focus in on emotional overload.

Emotional overload is caused by tension between the parents. Quarreling, complaining, and bickering between husband and wife stresses children by overloading them with fears and anxieties for which they may have no outlet. It is also produced by separation of any kind—being left with a babysitter, going to nursery or public school, going away to a camp for a couple of weeks, business travel of a parent, parental divorce or death. Some separation is normal, but too much separation can overstress a child and lead to symptoms of stress disease.[15]

Another contributing factor to emotional overload is being forced to adapt to change. Dr. Elkind gives a clear example: "Now consider Peter, a boy four years old. Both mother and father work and they have enrolled him in a full-day private nursery. In addition, because both parents have to leave home early, they have arranged to leave Peter with a neighbor, who will prepare him for the car pool person, who will take him to school before nine o'clock. After school, the car pool person drops him off at the neighbor's house again until his parents come to pick him up after work. By the time he gets home, Peter has been out of the house for almost twelve hours and has adapted to a number of different people (neighbor, car pool person, teachers)."[16] This takes the little boy right up to the limit of his emotional reserves.

The Perfect Crime—Molestation

The idea that adults might be sexually attracted to children is so offensive that most parents prefer not to think about it.

They should.

By conservative estimates, one out of ten children is sexually abused each year, often by a trusted authority figure—a teacher, doctor, or camp counselor—or by the parents themselves. In Pittsburgh a 24-year-old secretary is serving five years on probation for molesting the four-year-old girl for whom she babysat. A former mayor of Alamogordo, New Mexico, was convicted recently on five counts of sex crimes involving young girls. And a

Roman Catholic priest in charge of youth affairs at his church in suburban Los Angeles confessed to between 20 and 30 homosexual encounters with minors. Sexual child abuse cuts across all social, economic, and racial strata. Irving Prager, a California attorney who used to prosecute child molesters, believes that 'it is probably the most common serious crime against a person in the United States.'[17]

It's the perfect crime! In every respect, children are singularly vulnerable victims. They can be easily persuaded to cooperate with molesters and are then too afraid or ashamed to talk about it with their parents. Many parents believe their children will be safe if they don't talk to strangers. But in two-thirds of the cases victims and their parents know their assailants. A third of the victims are molested by a relative and an equal number by an acquaintance.[18]

The second major category of molestation is the "regressed offender." He is a man with a normal heterosexual orientation who turns to young girls at a crisis point in his life, such as a divorce or a professional setback. In Boston a 65-year-old widower with no previous history of child molestation was accused of fondling his neighbor's daughter, who brought over cookies to cheer him up after his wife died. Frequently, regressed offenders will suddenly begin to molest their own children. But the majority of men who commit incest do so because they are genuinely aroused by children.[19]

Most young victims of sexual abuse have been bribed or threatened not to talk about the experience. Molesters make a pact of secrecy with children, and that silence can be the source of their most intense suffering. Often it is far worse than the physical abuse. These aren't broken bones, but broken psyches! Children forced to keep their secret for any length of time may develop serious psychosomatic disorders—nightmares, insomnia, strange cramps, and stomachaches.[20]

Sex-abuse experts encourage parents to teach their children the difference between acceptable and unacceptable ways for them to be touched, as well as who has the right to touch them. Molesters are as threatening to children as drunk drivers, and children must learn how to avoid them, just as they learn to look both ways when they cross the street.[21]

Burnout

Just as adults experience a psychological or emotional burnout, children too suffer burnout from stress overload. Child burnout frequently brings about a sense of dissatisfaction with life. Nothing seems to be meaningful enough for the burned-out child. He can't sink his teeth into what to do with his life on a long-term basis. He also feels deprecated as a person of worth. Therefore, the child burnout detaches himself from intimate relationships.

Burnout children are extremely vulnerable people. Unable to stand alone, children who experience varying levels of burnout are most susceptible to the whims of their peer groups. What these whims may be doesn't really matter, because a burned-out child doesn't care anymore.

Little People Under Pressure
Become Big People

One of the most predominant characteristics of big people under pressure is that most of them were once little people under pressure! Stressed children many times grow bigger bodies in which to house their stress. The only difference is that the stress is probably a little more complex.

So what must we as parents do to help relieve our children's stressed state? Through extensive psychological testing, Thomas and Duazynski studied 1337 Johns Hopkins medical students who graduated between 1948 and 1964. They were trying to determine if there were predictable precursors of five disease states: suicide, mental illness, malignant tumor, hypertension, and coronary heart disease. The group who developed malignant tumors were the most psychologically distinct. *In all three groups, the "lack of closeness to parents" was the significant predictor of future disease.*[22] It's clear that parents must help the child cope with this pressure-cooker world primarily by a significant involvement in his life. We'll see how to do this in a later chapter.

STRESS TEST FOR KIDS

Children are stressed by all kinds of incidents—good, bad, and neutral. Measure your child's stress by counting up his or her various life-change-points that hurry and stress him. Add up the total points for all of the items your child has experienced in the last year. If your child scores below 150, he or she is about average with respect to stress load. If your child's score was between 150 and 300, he or she is above average and could begin to show some symptoms of stress overload. If above 300, there is a strong likelihood that he or she will experience a serious change in health and/or behavior.[23]

Stress Event	Value	Child's Score
Parent dies	100	
Parents divorce	73	
Parents separate	65	
Parent travels as part of job	63	
Close family member dies	63	
Personal illness or injury	53	
Parent remarries	50	
Parent fired from job	47	
Parents reconcile	45	
Mother goes to work	45	
Change in health of family member	44	
Mother becomes pregnant	40	
School difficulties	39	
Birth of a sibling	39	
School readjustment (new teacher or class)	39	
Change in family's financial condition	38	
Injury or illness of a close friend	37	
Starts a new (or changes) an extracurricular activity (music lessons, Brownies, etc.)	36	
Change in number of fights with siblings	35	
Threatened by violence at school	31	

Theft of personal
  possessions   30
Changes responsibilities at
  home   29
Older brother or sister
  leaves home   29
Trouble with grandparents   29
Outstanding personal
  achievement   28
Moves to another city   26
Moves to another part of
  town   26
Receives or loses a pet   25
Changes personal habits   24
Trouble with teacher   24
Change in hours with
  babysitter or at day-care
  center   20
Moves to a new house   20
Changes to a new school   20
Changes play habits   19
Vacations with family   19
Changes friends   18
Attends summer camp   17
Changes sleeping habits   16
Change in number of
  family get-togethers   15
Changes eating habits   15
Changes amount of TV
  viewing   13
Birthday party   12
Punished for not
  "telling the truth"   11

Is your child under pressure?

CHAPTER 6
The Battle of the Sexes

Unfortunately, too many male-female relationships go through three distinct stages. First it's the *ideal*. Then they go through an *ordeal*. Finally they each begin looking for a *new deal!* You see, if it weren't for marriage, husbands and wives would have to fight with strangers!

A woman called a lawyer and discussed her problems with her man. She asked, "Do I have grounds for divorce?" The lawyer replied, "Are you married?" "Of course!" The lawyer quickly responded "Then you have grounds for divorce!"

The battle of the sexes continues from the beginning of time. Much of the reason behind this great battle is the undying movement within every culture to attempt another homogenization process of male and female into a blend. In the fight for equality, differences fade or become blurred. Instead of the desired goal of equality (normally defined in a foggy manner), the final result is *sameness.* And the road leading to sameness has no arrival point, but is filled with holes of confusion—identity confusion! Male-and-female confusion!

In his classic work *The Decline of the West,* Oswald Spengler describes the inevitable rise and fall of all cultures with respect to the division of sexual labor. In ancient cultures the separation is great. The distinctions always become less and less with increasing culturization, and finally, when functional homogeneity is achieved, the end is at hand. The process of blending the male and female into one and the same is predictable and has occurred repeatedly in all cultural disintegrations of the past. Spengler's book was written in 1912![1]

Instead of two distinct yet equal sexes of male and female complementing each other, men and women are intensely competing with each other. When women see themselves in competition at home with their men, confusion reigns. All chiefs and no Indians! The result of this competition for "chief" equality is that no one ever wins. The rising emergence of the gay movement, along with the growth of all sexual problems, indicates how much our role reversals and confused sexual identities have become a way of life.[2]

MARITAL BATTLEFRONTS

After nearly 13 years of counseling, I have interfaced with thousands of the male and female varieties. My conclusion is that women are really weird and men are very strange (see Chapter 19). Because of their differing characteristics and identity confusion which fills the atmosphere, man and woman have "squared off" in opposition to each other. As a result, there are at least 11 marital battlefronts in the great battle of the sexes.

The Impossible/No Way Marriage

This battlefront is one of the toughest of all. This is when either husband or wife or both are unwilling to resolve the conflict that has broken the relationship. It's the common feeling that "I don't want to resume this relationship the way it is *and* I don't have any hope that it could get any better!"

This hopeless, give-it-up feeling is probably the

most common of all serious marital problems. No matter what is said, this is the heart of their feeling. As a counselor I quickly agree with the first part ("I don't want to resume this relationship the way it is . . ."), because in no way do I want their sick relationship to stay the way it is. But I adamantly disagree with the second part of the feeling ("I don't have any hope that it could get any better!")! In every male-female relationship there really isn't any hopelessness that cannot be fixed—except in the impossible/no way marriage.

This particular battlefront is the most lethal to any marriage, when a person follows both parts of the hopeless feeling. If a person stubbornly believes that it is hopeless to try to work out the problems in the relationship, then it is indeed impossible! It's an unfortunate state of affairs—like wearing emotional blinders to somehow escape the pain of confrontation.

Marriage Without a License

Another marital battlefront is when a man and woman practice marriage without a license. From the fear of marriage to the fear of divorce, the reasons vary for the experience of "living together." No matter what the reasons, in most cases living together as husband and wife without being husband and wife rarely works out positively!

Even though the only thing missing is a simple legal document, without that simple piece of paper complex and hurtful things happen. Normally the woman's confidence, trust, and respect for her man begin to erode. This erosion is evident through her feelings and expressions of insecurity and hostility. In her panic she critically picks away at her "lover's" inadequacies and smothers him with direct and indirect suggestions of marriage.

The man doesn't seem to be bothered by this loose-knit relationship. As a matter of fact, he likes it! It has all the benefits without the responsibility: it's risk free and he enjoys all levels of intimacy with very little commitment.

But both partners are losers. Although the woman has her man, she doesn't actually have her man at all. She has a male roommate or bed-partner, but the commitment dynamic is only one way—she is committed to him but he is "unable" to make his commitment yet. The man loses in that even though he has his cake and is eating it, his cake is in danger of spoiling or falling apart! Since most marriages without a license don't last long, everyone loses everything they wanted in the first place.

The Mind-Reader Marriage

This battlefront is saturated with unfulfilled and uncommunicated expectations. Expectations contain built-in disappointments, because expectations are, for the most part, unfounded. We are constantly hoping against hope or placing the opposite sex on a performance treadmill through our vain expectations.

There are two spin-off problems related to expectations. The first is the *active art of prediction*. This is a low-quality mind reading attempt. "If I had told you, you would have . . ." "But you wouldn't enjoy it!" When you try to read your man/woman's mind, you take away his/her freedom. No matter his track record of behavior in the past, it infuriates a person to be told what he would or wouldn't do, especially if his action was predicted to mess up something. As bad as this "skill" of mind-reading is in its own right, the worst problem is that this expectation is left unexpressed until after it's too late to do anything about the situation. It's used as a "Gotcha," a real zapper, in blaming someone else for your wrong behavior.

The second spin-off problem of expectations is just the opposite—the *passive art of protection*. Here the attempt is to protect yourself from having your mind read. It's having a hidden agenda in the relationship with invisible scoresheets. In fact, the only person who knows the rules of the contest is the person hiding the agenda.

Do you notice the basic universal ingredient within these two spin-off problems? They are both hiding or covering up true feelings. One of the primary reasons that we find it difficult to relate is that we have hidden expectations of one another. Until these are brought out into the open and discussed, there will be guerilla warfare. Expectations lose their destructive nature when openly expressed as desires and wants.[3]

Dictator—Doormat Marriages

A nasty rumor has been passed along for many years. The rumor is that the man is to be the dictator and the woman is to be *in her place* as the doormat. The man is to make all the decisions and the "dummy" wife is to quietly follow. This rumor has had devastating effects on marriages today!

When you think about it for a while, this plan is the most secure way to insure harmony and to eliminate conflict. You see, when only one person thinks and calls all the shots and the other hasn't had a thought in years, there will be no conflict. But there will be no marriage of two people, but only a small cult with its own eminent guru and his loyal, lonely follower!

In this battlefront neither the leader nor the follower is happy. Many times their behavior pattern is a way of protecting themselves from being responsible human beings who think, feel, and act. But each is angry with the other. He is angry with her lack of appreciation and respect, and she is angry with his lack of sensitivity and feeling for her. It's like a time bomb ticking away toward an inevitable explosion.

Parent-Child Marriages

It's so easy to slip into the parent-child marital battlefront. The most significant love relationship of the opposite sex is mom for a little boy and dad for a little girl.

In the marital relationship it's a natural slip for a man to marry his "mother" and a woman to marry her "father." The man usually acts like a mischievious child and his wife responds accordingly as the nagging mother. The woman who slips into the deviant pattern acts childish and spoiled, and her husband responds as her pampering father.

What makes this slip so destructive is that a man cannot make love to his mother and a woman cannot make her father her lover. This setup stunts mature growth—the man eventually feels emasculated and the woman begins to get feelings of nonfemininity. No one really wants to play these roles, but it's so comfortable to play "house" rather than real life!

Passive Men—Wild Women

This marital battlefront is a deadly cycle. When the man goes passive, his counterpart goes wild! This, in turn, makes the man go even more passive.

Although the man is active, articulate, energetic, and usually successful in his work, when he returns home he becomes inactive, inarticulate, and lethargic. He "turns out," becoming non-conversational, wolfing down his dinner, paying only token attention to his family and then withdrawing to the television set. He becomes passive. His wife, who has been wrapped up in her own problems all day, whether at home or in a career, is certainly looking for something more when her husband returns in the evening. She desperately wants to "tune in." She wants to talk, to share the experiences of his outside world, to get mental and physical reactions from him. But she isn't able to spark any of this, and in the face of his retreat into passivity, she goes "wild."[4]

Crowded Marriage

The phrase "Two's company and three's a crowd" is extremely applicable on this marital battlefront. Crowded marriages are everywhere.

There is the crowd of the married couple plus the in-laws. This crowded condition is caused by at least one of the members of the marriage remaining in psychological, if not financial, dependence upon mommy and daddy.

Then there is the crowd of the married couple plus their children. This crowd is caused by the children being the center and the prime reason for the couple's relationship. In this scene the male-female participants do not make a distinction between the marriage and the family. The marriage relationship must take priority over the family, because the stronger the marriage, the stronger the family. But if the family crowds out the marriage, the battle to come is inevitable in this crowded marriage.

Finally, there is the crowd of the married couple plus a third-party affair. This crowded condition is on the increase everywhere. Within the marriage both man and woman can become painfully lonely due to emotional isolation from each other. This sets up both man and woman with incredible needs, and they start looking for satisfaction. Then a third party enters with the same kind of loneliness and the same kind of needs. It's almost like two magnets being drawn together. This is called "love" or "I've never felt like this with anyone else before" or "I've learned how to communicate with feeling for the first time." But in nearly every case, it's not love, but the chemistry of two people feeling desperate need that any warm body can satisfy!

In each instance of the crowded marriage, the third party—in-laws, children, the magnetic opposite sex—successfully keeps the attention of man/woman away from his/her couple relationship to a temporary diversion. And in every situation the third party will not last long—in-laws die, children grow up, and affairs fizzle!

The Empty Marriage

This battlefront is subtle in its development. As the children are still at home, the couple's communication revolves almost entirely around their kids. But when they grow up and leave, the "empty nest" is so quiet that it's deafening.

But the empty marriage is also found *within* the man and the woman. It's most popularly called the midlife crisis. For the woman: she's intensely needed in the early years of marriage and the family. But as the kids move out, this woman is a "has-been." She's not needed anymore and she feels it deeply. Now panic sets in! She must do something for herself.

For the man: he drives and drives toward his goals. Again, as the kids are moving out, he wakes up to the fact that he has spent his entire life driving toward work goals. But he hasn't done a whole lot of living! He must now define his real desires in living and act them out before it's too late. What a strain this is on a marital relationship! This indeed is a stressful battlefront.

The Dual-Career Marriage

Career people are not just people with a career, but people who primarily live for their almighty careers. Career must take precedence over everything and everybody under the guise that all is done for everybody within the family. Career people aren't married to people but to their own careers!

One career person will destroy a male-female relationship, but a dual-career marriage never allows a relationship to happen at all. Dual-career people never really commit to marriage, and then are overwhelmed with shock over its failure.

The I'm-Not-in-Love-Anymore Marriage

This battlefront is certainly on the increase today.

It's a sort of "self con job." A person not getting his/her needs met wants out of the relationship but needs a good reason. Well, here is one of the best that almost anyone will accept as valid: "I love her, but I'm just not *in love* anymore." Anyone knows that if you are not *in love*, then your marital commitment is off the hook!

There is a twofold self-deception as to what the problem actually is. First, "not being in love anymore" often means that the infatuation is gone. But infatuation lacks the knowledge of the person being loved. Usually infatuation is a projected image of the person you *think* or *guess* or *hope* that he/she is. Infatuation, then, is not loving the real person, but loving your supposed projection of the person. This self-deception of infatuation is most frequent either early in a marriage or at any time when you are infatuated with someone else. Second, "not being in love anymore" also means that a person is unable or unwilling to communicate his/her wants and desires. And there *seems* to be no hope of opening up the lines of communication in a comfortable way.

The Great Sex Reversal

The great sex reversal is undoubtedly the most predominant and penetrating of the marital battlefronts. *Men are acting like women and women are acting like men.* This reversal emerges in two ways. One way is through a *confused sexual perspective.* The confusion lies within each person's makeup. Within each man is an inner female which enables him to have warm and meaningful human relationships. And within each woman is an inner male which gives her a desire for fulfillment in the area of goals and aspirations.

Understanding and expressing the inner capacities of the male and female are extremely helpful in the development of relationships. But there is a dark side to these inner counterparts that has the potential and the probability of destroying relationships. When the dark side of the man's inner female possesses and controls him, he becomes very moody (either hyped or depressed). His moods are totally irrational. He becomes overly sensitive, withdrawn and passive, and completely unavailable for relationships. When the dark side of the woman's inner male possesses and controls her, she becomes irrationally critical, judgmental, and opinionated. Her hostile dominance is riddled with "shoulds" for everyone. The man and his woman are two bitterly possessed people irrationally bruising each other. When the man is possessed by his female and the woman is possessed by her male, it's a royal sex reversal!

Another way the sex reversal emerges is through a *confusion in sexual preference.* When men act like women or are possessed by their dark-sided counterpart or when women follow the same pattern, their children are likely to be confused about their own sexual identity and their own sexual preference. A popular rumor within and about the gay movement is that homosexuality is a natural variant based on hormones. However, no remarkable endocrine alterations have ever been demonstrated in male homosexuals. Male homosexuals don't have unusual hormones. For modern man to justify his gayness on anything other than emotional grounds is contrary to the present knowledge available. The great sex reversal is an invisible destroyer of marital relationships behind all the previous battlefronts.[5]

The battle of the sexes will continue until the end of people. This battle is probably one of the most effective internal stresses of all. Since we cannot avoid the battle of competition, we must discover insights and action steps that will move us toward completion of each other.

CHAPTER 7
Your "Little Kid" Is Showing

Earlier, we reviewed the stress upon children when they are prematurely thrust into adulthood—*children living as miniature adults.* But there is another stressor as the kids actually grow to be adults—*adults living as giant kids.* Children are potentially dangerous animals—they become adults. But every adult was once a child and is a definite product of his/her childhood. Your childhood makes a distinct imprint on your life. In fact, you still have your "little kid" with you—your inner child of the past!

Somewhere, sometime, you were a child. This is one of the great and obvious, yet seemingly meaningless and forgotten, common denominators of adult life. The fact that you were once a child has an important bearing on your life today. In trying to be adults, we mistakenly try to ignore our lives as children, discount our childhood, and omit it in our considerations of ourselves and others. This is a way of mistreating ourselves.[1]

Whether you are now rich or poor, pleasantly satisfied with your lot or bitterly discontented, a homemaker or a career girl, married or divorced, in jail or in your own home, your childhood and the child you once were are not something wholly behind you, long ago and far away. Your childhood, in an actual, literal sense, exists within you now. It affects everything you do, everything you feel.[2]

These childhood feelings and attitudes influence,

often actually determine and dominate, your relations with friends, your colleagues, your mate, and even your own children. These feelings can interfere with your ability to work or to love. They may be a significant part of your fatigue, your inability to relax, your irritating headaches, or your upset stomach.[3]

Your "little kid" is showing every day through your various attitudes toward life.

PROCRASTINATOR/ DAYDREAMER/DAWDLER

The procrastinator/daydreamer/dawdler is a "little kid" showing. In addition to these subtle forms of resistance, this "little kid" is forgetful. This child needed encouragement to be a self-starter and to pursue his own interests. Instead, his/her parents most likely were overly coercive—directing, supervising, and redirecting. The child learned to quietly resist their coerciveness and develops this as a pattern for adulthood.

Another twist to this same profile is the bored adult. The child needed to be encouraged to be a self-starter and to pursue his own interests. This time the parents didn't overly coerce the child but were overly indulgent. Even before the child asked, wanted, or needed, the parents flooded him/her with things. The child's response was to develop a blasé attitude. Now he/she finds it very difficult to initiate anything and has little persistence in completing things.

PERFECTIONIST

A child has a need for productivity. It's the need to do, make, and accomplish things. But for anything to be completed as a production or creation, a child needs acceptance and appreciation from his parents. When parents withhold that acceptance and appreciation, the child is likely to develop the attitude that nothing is quite good enough, or it can always be better. This perfectionist profile is an inner child of the past!

DEMANDING

A child needs authoritative parents who will relate well but who will also make him/her responsible. This is especially true when a child makes his demands. He needs his parents to place limits and controls on his immature whims. But many times parents capitulate to the child's demands and whims. The child's response will be to become even more demanding with great outbursts of his temper.

IRRESPONSIBLE/IMPULSIVE/IMMATURE

This "little kid" is showing in epidemic proportions. A child needs a healthy relationship with the same-sex parent for development of conscience and personal identity. But when this relationship is missing, negative, or unhealthy, the child suffers greatly. Due to the hostility over the faulty or missing relationship with the same-sex parent, this "little kid" has great difficulty in maintaining long-term intimate relationships. This is the inner child that always wants to run away to avoid emotional pain.

LITTLE KIDS ARE EVERYWHERE YOU FIND ADULTS

Although we may not remember that child's

early feelings in our conscious memories, all of us, young or old, happy or unhappy, have unknowingly incorporated into ourselves the child we were. And that child is as alive and with us, and is as forceful a presence, as if he were living in our household. The very child that you were is buried within you, and even today he may be controlling the adult part of you. For when you, as an adult, are frightened, it's the child in you who is frightened, not the adult. When you appear to be angry, it's the child in you who is angry. When you are afraid to try, it's the child in you who is afraid to try. When you feel that you have to be good all the time to be loved, it's the little child within you, still looking for what you wanted so desperately when you were little.[4]

But what about the people who seem to be happy and functioning well? They seem to have gotten rid of their troublesome "little kid," but they have not. Their inner child is always with them with a latent zest for living. It's kind of a "personality pact" we all have with our inner child![5]

In all of us there is a child that wants to be soothed, caressed, cuddled, admired, repeatedly told that he is loved, and given constant reassurance that he will not be abandoned, negated, harmed, or destroyed. A child who is fortunate gets many of these responses from his mother. Many less fortunate ones do not. Later on we may get some of these responses from our fathers, siblings, grandparents, relatives, counselors, and friends. Our need for responses of this kind never ends. Even when we have had optimum responses in childhood, the child in us always requires a continuation of them.[6]

BE YOUR OWN PARENT

What each individual must be aware of is that his "little kid" needs someone to protect him from his own damaging feelings, and that he wants someone to assume responsibility for him and his very existence. Once the adult is willing to accept the responsibility for the well-being of his little child, he is accepting responsibility for his own well-being. He is making the decision to take care of himself. It's a decision to be your own parent![7]

As a child you naturally reacted to your parents' attitudes—and you still do, using these attitudes on yourself as an adult. Long before your adolescence you began a process of "internalizing" these attitudes, absorbing and integrating them into your way of considering, treating, and guiding yourself. During adolescence, when you gradually separated yourself from your parents' control, you began to be a parent to yourself.[8]

The various symptoms of your "little kid" are fairly obvious. They are all attitudes acquired from our parents or other significant relationships as a child. Instead of feeling like a victim to your upbringing and its resultant attitudes, you can and must effect appropriate changes—parenting your own "little kid."

In Dr. Hugh Missildine's helpful book, *Your Inner Child of the Past,* there is a useful table on how to parent yourself. It's not that specific nor is it complete, but is a helpful start to stimulate your thinking.

If in Childhood You experienced[9]	You can today
Perfection Overcoercion	Take off pressure and demands which you put on yourself.
Rejection Perfection Punitiveness	Put your emphasis on kindliness, respect, and gentleness in the way you treat yourself, and limit your self-criticism.
Overindulgence	Make demands on yourself to accomplish things; limit your dependence on others.
Oversubmission	Enforce firm limits on your impulsiveness, and work to overcome your tendency not to respect feelings and rights of others.
Neglect Rejection	Consciously do little kindnesses for yourself; indulge yourself when you can, and reduce your self-criticism.

Hypochondriacism   Refuse to give in to your
                                aches and pains.

When your "little kid" is showing off, don't neglect what's happening. Learn to be your own loving parent!

Thus far we have attempted to "picture the pressure"—both external and internal—that causes all the damaging and deadly stress in the family. Before moving on to some solutions to the many stressors destroying man and his family, there is one more basic picture of the pressure that is necessary. In a strange sort of way it's a picture of a person named Murphy!

CHAPTER 8
The Ultimate Source of Stress—Murphy! *

As a farmer walked across the field pulling a rope behind him, his friend asked, "What are you doing with that rope?" The farmer was startled momentarily and then said, "I don't know whether I lost my horse or found a rope!" Now that's confusion.

As has been demonstrated already, stress is basically the wear and tear of living life. The confusion and chaos we face daily are major contributors to our stressed world. More than anything else it's the fact that it's such a struggle to make life work!

Each day we awake to a world that appears more confused and disordered than the one we left the night before. Nothing seems to work anymore. Our lives are bound up in constant repair. We are forever mending and patching. Our leaders are forever lamenting and apologizing. Every time we think we've found a way out of a crisis, something backfires. The powers that be continue to address the problems at hand with solutions that create even greater problems than the ones they were meant to solve.[1]

There are accidents at nuclear power plants, killer carcinogens in the air and in most foods, the doubling and tripling of inflation figures, the steady loss of productivity and jobs, and the increased danger of thermonuclear war. Finally we want to roll down the window and scream out in despera-

*Portions of this chapter are adapted from Tim Timmons, *Loneliness Is Not a Disease* (Harvest House, 1981), Chapter 5.

tion, "Why isn't something being done about all
this!" We blame everybody and everything. We
blame the oil companies, the government econo-
mists, the unions, the family members, friends,
God, and anyone else we can target who's at all involved, and still things get worse![2]

Everywhere we go we find ourselves waiting in
lines or pushed into corners. Things about us continue to accelerate, yet nothing seems to be getting
anywhere. We are bogged down and the society is
bogged down. All of a sudden we get the urge to
trample over everything in our path, leaving the
world behind us in chaos. They tell us it's no better
anywhere else, and for once they're right! We look
at the other industrial societies, and while some appear worse off, and others slightly better off, all of
them, socialist and capitalist alike seem to be grip-
ped by a common malaise. The same degenerating
force of disintegration is eating away at all of us.[3]

ENTROPY: GOING DOWN HILL

Jeremy Rifkin's insightful work *Entropy* is a major
contribution to explaining why things seem to be
going downhill. He explains why progress, science,
and technology have not resulted in greater peace
and order but in fact in their very opposites: crisis,
chaos, pollution, and decay. By defining entropy in
simple terms he moves to apply this irreversible
law to every major arena of life.

Entropy is the second law of thermodynamics.
The laws of thermodynamics are the most basic
laws of science. All scientific fields are governed by
them. Therefore, these laws are inescapable! The
first law states that all matter and energy is constant in the universe, and it cannot be created or

destroyed. It can only be transformed, but not created or destroyed. We will never have any more or less matter and energy in the universe than we do now. The second law (entropy) states that, in the big picture, matter and energy can only be changed in one direction—from usable to unusable, from available to unavailable, from ordered to disordered. In essence, the second law says that everything in the entire universe began with structure and value but is irrevocably moving in the direction of randomness, chaos, and waste. In other words, entropy destroys the rumor that history is progress and the rumor that science and technology create a more ordered world.[4]

Every time matter and energy are transformed from one state to another, a price is paid for their use. That price is the loss of available matter and energy to perform any kind of work in the future. This loss and process of degeneration is entropy.

Every time something occurs in the natural world, some amount of energy ends up being unavailable for future work. That unavailable energy is what pollution is all about. Pollution is just another name for entropy. A human being, a skyscraper, an automobile, and a blade of grass all represent energy that has been transformed from one state to another. When a skyscraper or a blade of grass is formed, it's made of energy that has been gathered up from somewhere else. When the skyscraper is razed, and the blade of grass dies, the energy they embodied doesn't disappear. It is merely transferred back somewhere else into the environment.[5]

It is possible to reverse the entropy process in an isolated time and place, but only by using up additional energy; this then increases the overall entropy. Even recycling, which is extremely important, uses up more energy in the collection and processing of the used materials!

ENVIRONMENTAL ENTROPY

The energy crisis is for real—not just in oil and gas, but in all forms of energy. Energy needs will quadruple by the year 2000.[6] By the fact that our world is doubling every 35 years, the energy strain will continue exponentially. Between 1960 and 1975 the world's population grew at a rate of 2 percent per year, going from 2½ billion to 4 billion people. At current annual growth rates of 1.7 percent, the world's population will double to 8 billion by the year 2015 and to 16 billion by the year 2055. With this massive increase of people you can begin to understand the massive amount of energy that will be used up.[7]

TECHNOLOGICAL ENTROPY

In Jacques Ellul's *The Technological Society*, he criticizes the technocracy: "History shows that every technical application from its beginning presents certain unforeseeable secondary effects which are more disastrous than the lack of the technique would have been." He is speaking of the inescapable principle of entropy.[8]

The world is becoming more disordered because each time we apply a new and more complex technological solutions to a problem, it's like dousing a fire with gasoline. The more we technologize the world around us, the more things seem to malfunction and fall apart. The problems multiply faster than the solutions![9]

RELATIONAL ENTROPY

Because of entropy every aspect of our world experiences all forms of pollution. Our high standard of living is a massive energy flow and has a high price tag that accompanies it—the spreading of disease and death.

The law of entropy's pollution also penetrates into every relationship. Every relationship is governed by entropy. There is no exception. Each relationship—friend, business, marriage, and family—will fall apart and disintegrate if left to itself. There is a built-in fizzle in all relationships!

Human wreckage is a result of relational entropy. Failure within relationships has created piles of polluted people. These polluted people are disconnected and painfully detached from the life force of community. The desperate search for another relationship to fill the void of detachment is the motivating factor behind the family breakdown. Everyone is desperate for intimacy, but the price of becoming vulnerable is too painful to pursue.

Self-defeating solutions are everywhere. Arising out of a pervasive dissatisfaction with the quality of personal relationships, people are often advised not to make too large an investment or commitment in love and friendship, to avoid excessive dependence on others, and to live for the moment—the very conditions that created the crisis of lonely detachment in the first place.[10]

The pain of entropy's disintegration on the family is actually the pain of loneliness. In avoiding the pain of loneliness everyone seems to be looking for fast, temporary relief. It really doesn't matter what is used as the painkiller as long as it relieves the pain for now. It may be "self-awareness," "positive thinking," "success motivation," "holistic" lifestyle, EST, Lifespring, TA, TM, or maybe even pseudo-Christianity. Each of these is used as an aspirin, a high, a trip, or an anesthetic for the fast, temporary relief of pain.

IS MURPHY THE CULPRIT?

Man is falling apart at the seams. Each of us is literally going down hill—winding down, disintegrating, and degenerating right before the mirror! From pimples to wrinkles, gray hair to no hair, supple to sags and bags, and from intense activity to aches, creaks, and pains, *entropy is in force!* You can escape temporarily by eating properly and exercising regularly, but your body will continue to degenerate and someday "give up the ghost"— that's you!

Murphy has taken it upon himself to articulate the law of entropy and the downhill pull upon us all. I believe in Murphy and am a student of Murphology. You see, Murph tells it like it is! He writes about reality. Listen to a little Murphology:

If anything can go wrong, it will.

Nothing is as easy as it looks.

Everything takes longer than you think.

If there is a possibility of several things going wrong, the one that will cause the most damage will be the one to go wrong.

Left to themselves, things tend to go from bad to worse.

Whenever you set out to do something, something else must be done first.

If it's not one thing, it's another!

The other line moves faster.

The more boring and out-of-date the magazines in the waiting room, the longer you will have to wait for your scheduled appointment.

Murphy is absolutely right, but is he the cause of all this "reality?" I don't think so! He is just an unpopular commentator concerning the downhill trends.

FREEDOM: FACT OR FANTASY?
Entropy: The Ultimate Stressor

Life is a constant struggle to survive and to somehow reverse the irreversible law of entropy. This struggle is the ultimate source of stress. But even though everything and everyone is subject to entropy's grip, I believe there is hope to break free from its clutches.

Freedom is a wonderful thing. Most people have only the illusion of freedom. Some think they are free to love or hate anyone or to say or do anything they desire. But there is always a price tag. You are free to kill, but the price tag is prison or death. You are free to steal, to resent, or to hurt another person, but it will surely cost you. There is even the illusion of the "freedom to die." But that is not a freedom—that's a terminal prison!

There has never been a time in history in which the promise of freedom has been more prevalent—and marketable. Promise of life, power, sex appeal, fame, leisure, freedom to be, and success are found in every corner of our society. Yet people have never experienced less freedom, with all of our impotence, boredom, lostness, and hassled lifestyle. Never have people been so shackled, possessed, controlled, addicted, paralyzed, anxious, or obsessed as they are today! It's all a fantasy of freedom.

Freedom's Limitations

The great historian Will Durant expressed it well when he said, ''The first condition of freedom is its limitations.'' For the most part man has limited his freedom to himself. That's not freedom because man has a terminal illness—he's in the process of dying! You limit yourself to man if man is God, and you worship a very sick God.

Man is basically not O.K.! Man is in trouble. No matter how many ways man is not O.K. becasue he is not normal in his present state. He is abnormal.

For me, the most reasonable explanation for man's abnormal state is in the Bible. Man was created perfect and complete. He was normal in his original state. But through his rebellion against his Creator, man became abnormal. In his normal condition ''man and his wife were both naked and not ashamed.'' They had total communication and intimacy, free from inhibitions. After man's rebellion he hid himself from his Creator and his mate. He felt alienation, fear, and pain for the first time. He realized that he was definitely not O.K.!

If man today were normal by not being O.K., then there would not be much hope of man getting any better. However, since man's state is *abnormal* today, there is hope for positive change—to move back toward normality. So man, once O.K., is not O.K. now, but has the hope of being O.K. in the future! So, I'm not O.K., you're not O.K., and that's O.K. because there's hope!

The only hope for true freedom from the entropy law of death and dying is to limit yourself to something or someone that is free from that law. *To be fully free from death and dying (entropy) you must commit yourself to be limited only by God and His principles.* If God is your only limitation, you are free!

But man is still rebelling. He says, "God, You go Your way and I'll go mine. Check with me when I'm 76 or 77, and we'll negotiate then!" The process goes something like this: little boy believes in Santa Claus. As he grows up, he doesn't believe in Santa Claus. Then, when fully grown, he believes he *is* Santa Claus! The same is true concerning God. As a youngster, man believes in God. As he grows up, he doesn't believe in God. Then, when fully grown, he believes he *is* God! But to be fully free man must commit himself to be limited only by God and His principles.

A kid reporter happened to be the only reporter from his paper on the scene at the Johnstown Flood in 1889. He was so excited about this opportunity that he was caught up in the magnitude of it all. He telegraphed his report back to his editor. It read: "God sits broodingly on the hillside overlooking the disaster and desolation of Johnstown. The roaring waters seem to echo the mind of the Creator..." His editor immediately telegraphed back to the kid: *"Don't limit youself to the flood. Interview God!"*

Don't limit yourself to man. Limit yourself only to God and His principles. That's true freedom! Check it out in Part Two.

Part Two
Process the Pressure

CHAPTER 9
Don't Stuff It—Process It!

A tailor was having difficulty getting to sleep at night, so his friend suggested, "You need to count sheep. That will put you to sleep!" Optimistic, the tailor went home expecting to finally get some sleep. But the next day he came into his shop looking worse than he had for weeks. When his friend saw his worsened condition, he asked, "What went wrong? Didn't you count sheep, as I suggested?" The tailor said, "I tried it. I counted sheep. I counted up to 3000 sheep! But when I got to 3000 sheep, I realized that many sheep would translate into 8000 yards of wool, which would be able to produce 2500 suits. So I worried the rest of the night where I was going to find the lining to go in all those suits!" To one person, counting sheep soothes him, but to another person those same sheep stress him. Each person may be stressed differently, but each person *is* stressed.

Now that we have a picture of the stress that is repeatedly overcharging all of our bodily systems and damaging our family relationships, we must learn *how to live through it.* We cannot avoid stress, because it's a part of living. We cannot effectively *retreat* from it. There is no *repellent* available.

Skillful repression or angry *reaction* against the stressors inevitably produce even more stress.

One of the most alluring factors to me about the Bible is its realism. It's true to life as it is and people as they are. There is no cover-up of people's failures and no promise of material wealth or continuous good health, but a description of real people living their lives connected to their God and practicing His principles of life.

His principles of life are true no matter what you think or believe about them. They're like the laws of nature. For instance, there is the principle of gravity. Stated simply, this principle says that if you jump off a two-story building, you'll come down fast and hit with a thud. And you probably won't like it! It doesn't make any difference what you think or believe about it, or whether or not you like it. The principle is true. Even if the principle of gravity were placed on a national ballot and voted down unanimously, the next person who attempted to jump off a two-story building would find that the principle didn't know it had been voted out of existence. As he jumped, he would come down fast and hit with a thud.

When you follow the principles of life, you'll experience personal fulfillment. But if you ignore these principles, you'll experience everything but personal fulfillment.

You don't have to understand life's principles to follow them. I don't understand how electricity works, but I flip the switch and read by the light. I don't understand how a brown cow can eat green grass and make white milk and yellow butter, but I eat all of it except the grass! Principles are true no matter what level of understanding you have of them.

The principles of life can govern your life toward maximum fulfillment of who you are! There are principles of lifestyle that relate to you alone, to you and your relationships, and to you and your vocation. These principles of life are vital in understanding how a marriage works.

After much searching I have found that one book contains these vital principles of life. (It's not one of mine.) Let me give you the title. It's BIBLE! Now before you panic, let me explain what I mean.

On a flight from New York to Los Angeles, an executive sat down next to me. After a few conversational cliches he asked, "What do you do?"

I quickly replied, "I speak."

He said, "I know that, but what do you do for a living?"

Again I said, "I speak!"

"On what?" he continued.

"Well, I speak on lifestyle, marriage, parenting, long-term selling and managing, and so on."

He seemed interested. "Really! Are you a psychiatrist?"

"No," I replied, "but I have a psychiatrist who works with me."

"Well, then," he said, "are you a psychologist?"

"No, I'm not one of those either, but I do have two of them who work for me."

Then in a somewhat frustrated manner he said, "Well, what are you?" It hurts a little bit when someone asks, "What are you?" but I bounced back with "I'm just a speaker!" Now that my profession was established, he started on his second set of 20 questions.

"Where do you get your material?"

If I told him he probably wouldn't believe me, I said.

"No," he said, "come on, where do you get your stuff?"

So I told him, "I get it out of a book."

"In a book! What's the title of the book?"

I had him get out his pen. He fumbled for a minute and finally got his pen and datebook in hand to receive the title of my resource book.

Calmly I announced, "The title of the book is Bible."

He seemed a little stunned with my answer and said in a rather loud voice, "Bible? You get your material to speak to corporations from the Bible? What is there to talk about in the Bible?"

I'd heard that question so many times in similar situations that I was ready for it. "Oh," I said, "I speak quite a bit on sex!"

He choked slightly, "From the Bible?" His shock came from a common misconception that the Bible says, "Thou shalt not!" about sex. It actually says "Thou shalt!" and it even goes so far as to say, "Thou shalt enjoy it, when thou shalt!"

"Oh, yes, from the Bible!" I assured him. "There are all kinds of principles of life concerning sex in the Bible. Moses wrote in Deuteronomy 24:5 that when a man gets married, he shouldn't be drafted into the military or work, but he should cheer up his wife for a year. I can't explain it all right now, but that Hebrew word for 'cheer up' doesn't mean to tell jokes for a year. It's referring to sex!"

Now the inquisitive executive began to take notes. "Now, where is that verse?" Can't you just see him going to his hotel room and pulling out the Gideon Bible from the nightstand drawer? Principles of life are universal principles, and no matter where you find them, people want them. That's because they are true to people as they are and life as it is.

It's none of my business what you live by or what you think about the Bible. I feel like the Toyota commercial: "If you can find a better car, buy it!" If you can find a better source for principles of life that are true to people as they are and life as it is, then you better buy it!

PROCESSED LIFESTYLE

The Biblical lifestyle is portrayed as a person depending upon God, living life wisely or foolishly, and experiencing the subsequent consequences. Within this lifestyle man can affect his own destiny significantly and positively by *responding properly to God and His principles for living.*

Instead of retreating, repelling, repressing, or reacting, try *responding. Responding is the art of facing whatever comes with God's power and your practice.* You see, *responding is processing!*

The most important ingredient in responding or processing is *wanting to change.* When it's all said and done, you do primarily what you really want to do. In order to process the pressures of life you must have a desire to change and you must make a decision to change. That's what growth and maturity are all about.

I almost forgot the key of keys to processing the pressure. You may desire to change and make a decision to change, but if you don't do something about it there is no change. If there are six birds on a fence and five of them decide to fly away, how many birds are still on the fence? You're right! There are still six birds on the fence, because just deciding to fly away doesn't mean you actually do it! Processing demands the desire to change, the decision to change, and the actual doing of it.

There are five foundational action steps to help you process the pressure. Each of these steps requires a great desire, a definite decision, and a lot of doing. Let's get on to the process.

CHAPTER 10
*Learning to Be a Lover**

Our world is full of crises, but the greatest of these is a *love crisis*. It's a crisis because of the mass confusion over the little four-letter word *love*. Love is one of the most overworked words in the English language; some dictionaries list as many as 25 meanings of love! Just having one word for everything leads to confusion and strange comparisons. For example, we love our lifelong sweetheart. But we also love fried chicken or quiche Lorraine, thus comparing our marriage partners of 30 years to a French cheese pie! We love our parents and our children. But we also love books or football or skiing vacations. We love freedom, which is surely more precious than the shiny machine in the driveway. But we *love* that new car; we also love our pets and a certain record album we bought last week. It all adds up to confusion over love—a love crisis! It's difficult to love when the meaning of love is so fuzzy.[1]

Even though the difficulty of loving is great, the very first step in processing your pressure is learning to be a lover. It's not learning how to get others to love you—to be loved in a passive sense—but actively learning to be a lover. In order to effectively process the pressure you must know where to shoot, rather than just babbling and weaving and ducking all of the stress bombardment.

*Portions of this chapter are adapted from Tim Timmons, *Loneliness Is Not a Disease* (Harvest House, 1981), Chapter 8.

The Bible sets forth principles of love that plug people into life. There is no greater Biblical passage concerning the life principles of love than found in the first letter Paul wrote to the Corinthians. He articulately defines true love—its absence, presence, and permanence:

THE ABSENCE OF TRUE LOVE

If I speak with the tongues of men and of angels, but do not have love, I have become a noisy gong or a clanging cymbal. And if I have the gift of prophecy, and know all mysteries and all knowledge; and if I have all faith, so as to remove mountains, but do not have love, I am nothing. And if I give all my possessions to feed the poor, and if I deliver my body to be burned, but do not have love, it profits me nothing (1 Corinthians 13:1-3).

THE PRESENCE OF TRUE LOVE

Love is patient, love is kind,
and is not jealous;
Love does not brag and is not arrogant,
does not act unbecomingly;
it does not seek its own,
is not provoked,
does not take into account a wrong suffered,
does not rejoice in unrighteousness,
but rejoices with the truth;
bears all things,
believes all things,
hopes all things,
endures all things.
Love never fails (1 Corinthians 13:4-8).

THE PERMANENCE OF TRUE LOVE

But if there are gifts of prophecy, they will be done away; if there are tongues, they will cease; if there is knowledge, it will be done away. For we know in part, and we prophesy in part; but when the perfect comes, the partial will be done away. When I was a child, I used to speak as a child, think as a child, reason as a child; when I became a man, I did away with childish things. For now we see in a mirror dimly, but then face to face; now I know in part, but then I shall know fully just as I also have been fully known. But now abide faith, hope, love, these three; but the greatest of these is love (1 Corinthians 13:8-13).

LOVE FILLS THE VACUUMS

There are six basic principles which explain the dynamic of true love. The first of these is best seen when love is absent: *True love fills inner vacuums.* The loneliest place in the world is the human heart when love is absent. Without love, spiritual communications ("If I speak with the tongues of men and of angels") are not important. They have become a noisy gong or a clanging cymbal. Without love, great giftedness, many talents, and vast knowledge—even powerful faith—position you as *nothing.* Without love, sacrificial gifts and martyrdom profit nothing.

Love can dynamically fill up the vacuums and fill in the gaps as needed in relationships. When things are falling apart, love can put them back together. When things go wrong, love can make them right. When people are hurt, love can heal.

Communication gaps that exist between parents and their children can be bridged only by true love. Parents may discipline their children toward perfection, but without an adequate expression of love, even consistent and proper discipline tends to push the child's rebellion button. On the other side, if parents develop a love relationship with their children but "blow it" in discipline, they will still have a good chance of being successful in parenting.

In the counseling room the absence of love is the major reason for the problem, no matter what you call it. That is why the truly successful counselor (whether professional or nonprofessional) communicates love for the counselee. Ninety percent of the problem is solved by the counselor's expression of love—"I care that you get through this." Why? Because *true love fills inner vacuums*.

GIVING AWAY LOVE

The second basic principle in the blueprint for true love is: *True love is a free gift for the givee*. Love is primarily giving, not receiving. Love may be expressed conditionally or unconditionally. Healthy love works when love is given as an unconditional, free gift. There are no strings attached and no treadmills built. It is only in the atmosphere of unconditional, true love that the blockages can be torn down and the blurs cleared up within the relationship.

The Greek word used for love in the Biblical blueprint is *agape*. Agape is an act of the will toward an unconditional expression of love. Agape love doesn't just verbalize, but mobilizes into action. It's something you do for someone. *True love must be given away.* It's a commitment toward promoting the well-being of another person.

My love must empower you to love yourself. Our success in loving is judged not by those who admire us for our accomplishments, but by the number of those who attribute their wholeness to our loving them, by the number of those who have seen their beauty in our eyes and heard their goodness acknowledged in the warmth of our voices. We are like mirrors to one another. It's an absolute certainty that no one can know his own beauty or perceive a sense of his own worth until it has been reflected back in the mirror of another loving person.[2]

As the blueprint for true love states, "Love does not seek its own." It is not *self*-centered but *other*-centered! For years I wanted my wife to play the normal sports with me—like tennis, basketball, etc. But I was extremely unsuccessful; she wanted to play things like hiking! To me hiking is just aimlessly wandering through the woods. But my attitude was getting nowhere.

So I decided to unselfishly love my wife in this small slice of our lives together. I came home one day and said, "I want to go hiking with you!" Obviously stunned, she said, "Hiking! You want to go *hiking?*" From that day forward Carol has even wanted to play some of the more-normal sports! *True love does not seek its own, but seeks the best for the one loved.*

The risk in committing yourself to unconditionally loving someone is very high. You take the risk of giving love as a free, unconditional gift and not receiving anything at all in return. That's a heavy risk, and yet without such a risk there is no reward and no relief of the pain of loneliness.

THE PRICE OF TRUE LOVE

The third basic principle is: *True love has a price tag for the giver.* The price tag is very high. For some people the price tag seems too high! The price tag calls for the giving of yourself. True love involves the willingness to face the inevitable pain, doubt, confrontation, misunderstanding, and dark moments within relationships. The price tag demands that you face the relationship yourself. It demands vulnerability. People love because they are afraid of themselves, afraid of the loneliness that lives in them. People need someone in whom they can lose themselves as smoke loses itself in the sky.

To restate the principle simply: *You must lose yourself in order to find yourself; you must die to yourself in order to really live.* True love cannot happen in a vacuum but only in relationship—an interdependent relationship. This may be the most radical principle of true love. When you give all that you know you are into a relationship, you mysteriously discover a more healthy *you.* Your self-image is directly connected to the quality of your relationships with other people.

LOVE THAT FREES

The fourth basic principle of true love is: *True love is affirmation rather than possession.* The question is whether your love is possessive and manipulative or really affirming and freeing. What is more important—that a person is pleased with himself or that you are pleased with him? Wanting what is best for another person and trying to be what that person needs you to be can be done only in a way that preserves his freedom to have his own feelings, think his own thoughts, and make his own decisions. True love is the affirmation and the celebration of an unrepeatable miracle—the uniqueness of the person loved.[3]

The Biblical blueprint for true love is entirely designed to affirm. The qualities listed in 1 Corinthians 13 all seem to follow the two themes of patience (having a long fuse) and kindness (doing good toward another person). Love in the form of patience is an uncommon power to cope with common suffering. Suffering itself takes no talent; it comes to us, takes us captive, pins us down. We are all its victims. Some of us have to suffer more than others. Some of us are able to suffer with more grace than others. But it is love that enables us to suffer long. It is having to endure what we very much want not to endure. On the other hand, kindness is the work of the power of love. Kindness is the will to save. It is love acting on persons. Such kindness may be soft, but it is not weak; tender, but not feeble; sensitive, but not fragile.[4]

Patience	Kindness
. . . is not jealous	. . . does not brag and is not arrogant
. . . is not provoked	. . . does not act unbecomingly
. . . does not take into account a wrong suffered	. . . does not seek its own
. . . bears all things	. . . does not rejoice in unrighteousness, but rejoices in the truth
. . . endures all things	. . . believes all things
	. . . hopes all things

Being patient and kind toward a loved one is actually joining that person's team. And we all desperately need team members who are a reservoir of strength against the killer of loneliness.

TRUE LOVE FOREVER

Love's *absence* can be devastating. Its *presence* is extremely supportive. But its *permanence* is its most distinctive characteristic. The fifth principle of true love is: *True love is a taste of eternity.* In our world of the handy, disposable "throwaways," the forever-ness of love is most rare!

The Biblical blueprint in 1 Corinthians 13:8-13 calls for everything as we know it to stop or run out someday. The only things in this world remaining throughout eternity are faith, hope, and agape love.

There is no time limit on love. To place a limit of any kind on love makes love conditional. The commitment of love, at whatever level, has to be permanent, a lifetime wager. If I say that I am your friend, I will always be your friend, not "as long as" or "until" anything. Effective love is not like the retractable point on a ball-point pen. I need to know that the love you offer me is a permanent offer before I will give up my security operations, my masks, my roles, and my games. I cannot come out to a temporary, tentative love, to an offer which has all that fine print in the contract.[5]

MAKING LOVE WORK

The final basic principle in the Biblical blueprint for true love is: *True love is an active process.* No matter how romanticists have tried to color it ever-sweet, and despite the claim of cynics that it is overrated, love is the tough, essential answer to the riddle of human existence, of human wholeness and happiness. To live is to love. But if love really is the answer, it seems quite certain that the efforts of humans to find this answer in love relationships have a high mortality rate. *Love works only if people work at it!*[6]

The Biblical blueprint for true love sets the standard so high that it seems humanly impossible. Unconditional, agape love is an ideal—a goal toward which true love aspires. True love requires constant work. It's a full-time job!

True love is also a process. You can never arrive. There are no push-button answers or quickie formulas or instant miracles that will switch love to a natural, automatic pilot. Most people are looking for miracles, but life is really a process. That's what true love is all about—a lifelong process!

INABILITY TO LOVE?

The more people I counsel, the more I am convinced that most do not have the basic capability to love truly. Jesus offered helpful insight into this problem when He was asked, "Teacher, which is the greatest commandment in the Law?" He answered, " 'You shall love the Lord your God with all your heart and with all your soul and with all your mind.' This is the great and foremost commandment. The second is like it: 'You shall love your neighbor as yourself.' " (Matthew 22:36-39).

The theme of God's communication to man is love. I like that! I also like it because Jesus did not answer the question and stop, but answered the question and added to it. By this addition He completed what true love is all about. It's more than loving your fellow man or woman (neighbor). It's loving God and loving yourself!

GOD—I LOVE YOU!

In order to develop the *ability to love*, we must

first love God. This is not loving *what God does,* but loving *who He is.* You see, if you can't accept who God is, you won't accept what God does! After receiving God's love for us, we are to reciprocate love back to Him.

One of the greatest roadblocks to loving is self-centeredness—selfishness. Selfishness is simply a pride that likes playing God. The opposite is to let God be God and love Him for it.

When our focus is turned inward, it is impossible to give ourselves effectively to much of anything. When turned inward, we wallow with the friends of pride: loneliness, guilt, anger, resentment, depression, physical pains, pity, and, of course, stress. But if we can focus outside ourselves, there is a freedom to break out of our spell of living life all by our panicky selves.

Loving God will translate you out of yourself into a more healthy you, capable of truly loving somebody else. There is something about the spiritual exercise of loving God—talking to Him (praying to God), listening to Him (studying Him), and pleasing Him (conducting your life according to His principles for living)—that will move you out of your selfishness and yet at the same time fill you up and turn you on as a person. You see, everything works best when it's plugged in! By actively loving God, you plug yourself into love and life.

I LOVE ME!

Jesus offered a second dynamic in developing the ability to love: "Love your neighbor as yourself." You must love yourself. According to this principle, if you don't love yourself, your neighbor's in a heap of trouble! And neighbors *are* in trouble because it is extremely rare for people to love themselves.

Self-love is not the same as selfishness. Selfishness is a kind of greediness which cannot be satisfied. It's a bottomless pit of restless envy of others and a subtle self-hate. In other words, selfishness is the very opposite of self-love.

You are the very creation of God—created in the image of God. In fact, you are an unrepeatable miracle! No one else in this world is like you. There is no comparison. You're not in the same ball game with anybody else in the world, because you are truly unique. Instead of loving and celebrating ourselves, we are too busy comparing, competing, and conforming to others or to a fantasy image of something we are not.

If you could absorb all the facts about you, you would pat yourself on the back and celebrate your specialness every day. Let me share just one of these facts: when your father deposited 10 million to 2 billion sperm into your mother, they were all after your mother's egg. Now which one of these 2 billion sperm got your mother's egg? *You* did! You won! *You won in a "footrace" against 2 billion others!* Isn't that incredible? You ought to congratulate yourself! You were Number One. Nobody is like you anywhere!

In this chapter we've seen what true love of another person is and the two dynamics—*I love God* and *I love me*—which develop the capability of expressing true love to another person. Why not try exercising these two dynamics over the next few weeks? When you get up in the morning, instead of saying "Good God, it's morning!" try "Good morning, God! I love You today!" Then as you sneak up on your bathroom mirror in the morning, look into that mirror (make certain you are alone) and say to yourself with enthusiasm, "Self, I love you!" Try this simple exercise that many others have and watch your behavior change! I dare you!

CHAPTER 11
Handling Your Hurts

Sticks and stones may break your bones, but words may destroy you! These may be nothing more stressful than the criticisms, insults, and rejections that human beings must experience. Unfortunately, most people react to these hurts by stuffing them in their gut rather than handling the hurts responsibly. People deceive themselves into the "shortcut" method of dealing with their hurts, only to discover that they have chosen the longest way to healing instead.

THE CRICITAL SHOULDS
Perhaps the most common hurt occurs through the wear-and-tear stress of the critical "shoulds," both spoken and unspoken. So many people live in the claustrophobic boxlike shadow of somebody else's "shoulds." "Shoulds" leave no room for expression of personal uniqueness, for individual decisions, or for personal freedom.

Besides the great loss of free individual expression, the hurts happen primarily in two ways. First, the depression hurts deeply. The normal first reaction to someone's critical "should" is to *deny* any wrongdoing. From there it is *blame*. When denial doesn't work, then blame someone or something—quickly! The reaction now moves to *anger*. But instead of expressing the anger, most people stuff it into *depression*. That depression can easily become depression overload, and that can be fatal.

DON'T DEHUMANIZE ME

Several studies have demonstrated that in order to totally reject someone you must dehumanize the person. Police have to view a criminal as an animal or a thing in order to shoot or attack the "bad guy." A person cannot divorce a human being. He/she must view the other person as a bear or a machine or a monster, but not a real, live person.

How many times have you rejected someone and possibly resented him/her with "good reason," and then actually met with the person and humanly related to him/her? Then you realized that he/she wasn't so bad after all! What happened? That person was an animal or a thing and then mysteriously was transformed into a human being!

But what caused this transformation? Instead of reacting against the person or resenting the person, the decision was made to *relate person to person!*

HANDLE YOUR HURTS BY RELATING

When you are confronted with verbal darts of insults, criticisms, or rejection, it's very possible that you need to change. In other words, your "oppressor" could be right! He may lack tact in how to communicate his criticism, but in substance he just could be right. Maybe you lacked needed information and acted accordingly, but with the new info you definitely want to change your action. Change is always a part of growth.

But much of the criticism that hurts offers no specific suggestion as to what to do. Remember, nothing is impossible for the person who doesn't have to do it. So few critics offer what to do differently, but "just do it." A good question in response to this kind of criticism is to ask, "How would you do it?" or "What would you suggest that I do differently?" This shows a willingness to change. That attitude in itself will be disarming to most of your critics.

Consider the Source

The credibility of your critic is very important. A childless person criticizing your parenting style may not know what he/she is saying. It's like a bald man selling hair tonic or an insurance salesman who owns none. Always consider the source.

Don't be too quick to either accept or reject your critic's words. You may really need to change, or you might just be listening to a fool. *Never argue with a fool, because it's so hard for other people to tell the difference.* You can recognize a fool because he is usually lazy, irresponsible, mouthy, prone to gossip, and impulsive. He talks a great game, but his life is filled with a track record of wreckage. Don't listen to his criticism.

There is also the critic who is well-meaning, but is without knowledge. Unfortunately, we live in a world in which it is so very important for everyone to have an opinion about everyone else. This forces people to become opinionated, either positively or negatively, without necessarily knowing anything about the subject. Either fill in your critic on his misinformation or lack of information, or else discount his criticism as being ignorant. But whatever you do, handle that possible hurt and don't allow it to fester.

Still another possibility, when considering the source, is to ask, "What does my critic really want?" Many critics don't really care what you do or don't do, but rather whether you care for them or not. What many critics are desiring from their targets is attention or appreciation of them. When realizing this, I have been able to dissolve many critics and avoid any hurt to me or to others.

Be careful when discounting your critic's criticism. You may end up discounting the critic as you discount the criticism. Discounting your critic starts the cycle of hurting all over again, except that this time *you* are doing the shooting of the darts and *he* is doing the hurting. Now we have great potential for miniwarfare.

Even in discounting the criticism, do it positively. Look for something you can use, even within negative, off-the-wall criticism. I don't know of anything better in handling criticism (and life, for that matter) than the philosophy of the cherry. It is: *eat the cherry and spit out the pits!*

Counteract with a Blessing

To handle your hurts, *changing* and *considering the source* are effective, but neither is as life-changing as *counteracting with a blessing.* The most natural reaction to a hurtful verbal dart is to shoot back. But that reaction only serves to produce even more stress in the scenario. A Biblical passage speaks directly to this. Peter, who had quite a reputation for being a reactionary talker, put it this way:

To sum up, let all be harmonious, sympathetic, brotherly, kindhearted, and humble in spirit; not returning evil for evil, or insult for insult, but giving a blessing instead; for you were called for the very purpose that you might inherit a blessing.

For, let him who means to love life and see good days

Refrain his tongue from evil
and his lips from speaking guile.
And let him turn away from evil and do
good;
Let him seek peace and pursue it.
For the eyes of the Lord are upon the
righteous,
And His ears attend to their prayer,
But the face of the Lord is against
those who do evil (1 Peter 3:8-12).

When you have been hurt, giving a blessing instead of an insult is a tall order! Although extremely
difficult to execute, there are two very good reasons
for trying it. First, giving a blessing is a total surprise. It's the shock method! No one expects this
kind of positive response. Taken off guard, your attacker finds it difficult to keep on attacking.
Secondly, there is a special blessing of God for the
one giving a blessing. Conversely, He is against
those reacting with an insult.

We are all so good at handing out insults, sar-
casm, and ridicule, and are basically blessed with
the ability of harming people verbally. I'm certain
that I have a spiritual gift in this area! You can hurt
people by attacking a weakness or predicting
motives, by silence or clamming up, and by
absence. One of the most popular methods is the
hit-and-run method of conflict. This is the urge to
get in the last word and walk off or slam the phone
down. All of these methods do their best to destroy
every level of endearment in a relationship.

Giving a blessing is speaking praise or thanks-
giving for someone. It's speaking well of him or her
with a positive, encouraging word. It is a statement
of healing. But how you give a blessing will make or
break effectiveness.

For years I have counseled people to handle their hurts by counteracting with a blessing, and it works wonders for both the "blesser" and the "blessee." I suggest following the four steps that Jesus took when counteracting with a blessing (see 1 Peter 2:21-24).

1. *Give no offense.* When giving a blessing, be doubly sure that you are not in the wrong. Otherwise your blessing will be nullified. Carol and I were in the bathroom getting ready for the day. All of a sudden she started shooting at me verbally. I waited a few moments and came back at her with a blessing. I told her how much I appreciated her. She quickly said, "If that was meant to be a blessing, it isn't going to work!" I was in shock. She then proceeded to explain to me how I had verbally insulted her earlier in the morning. I was unaware of what I had done. (I told you it may be a gift!) But believe me when I say that it doesn't work to give a blessing and be an offender at the same time!

2. *Give no reaction.* When hurt, don't get caught up in emotional reaction against your aggressor. It will lead to more struggle and more hurt. As a matter of fact, to your aggressor, it "proves" without a doubt that you deserved everthing he shot at you, and more.

3. *Give it over to God.* It's so easy to play God in relationships and take your own revenge against someone who has wronged you. But there is no profit—not even adequate retribution for your hurt. There is rarely, if ever, a sense of satisfaction in "getting back."

One of my favorite Biblical principles is, "Never take your own revenge, but leave room for the wrath of God, for it is written, 'Vengeance is mine,

I will repay, says the Lord' " (Romans 12:19). In other words, scoot over and let God deal with your attacker. He'll do a much better job anyway. That's giving it over to God!

4. *Be willing to hurt in order to heal.* When you give a blessing, all may not be resolved right away. In fact, you may look like the fool or feel rejection because of your position of blessing. Giving a blessing is no magic formula for instant relief. You may find that your hurt may never be satisfied or "paid for." Be willing to hurt in order to heal. Which is more important—healing for you and your offender or that your hurt has been paid back? In the long run there is no question as to which is more important and beneficial for everyone.

Let's look in on Cindy. Her husband has hurt her repeatedly with his sharp and cutting tongue. Now on top of all this Bob has decided to take a little time out for his own midlife crisis. He wants some space—time to think things over and to play with a young honey in his office. At first Cindy isn't aware of his young friend, but begins to suspect something. When he does finally admit that his "space" is a little crowded, Cindy experiences one of the most acute hurts known to mankind.

Cindy came in for some advice on how to leave Bob in a "Christian" sort of way. She was so hurt that she had shut down any positive feelings of love for Bob. I suggested that she could *really* work Bob over by giving him a blessing. She laughed so hard at my choice of words that she shifted down into her real feelings and had a hard cry! Now she was ready to "work Bob over."

We listed the kinds of blessings she could give him and the four-step how-to. She tried it and tried it. It seemed like nothing was going to penetrate or interrupt Bob's crisis. Cindy felt better already because she was acting as a healing agent. That's a healthy position. This pose is also very alluring, especially to a man having his own personal midlife crisis! Bob didn't even know what was happening to him. He was drawn back to his senses by a blessing. She was willing to hurt, with all its embarrassment and pain, in order to heal both sides of the relationship. And it worked!

CAN'T OR WON'T

Either handle your hurts or be handled by them. At this point I can hear many objections like, "But you don't understand!" or "You just don't know how painful it is!" or "If I gave a blessing, he'd step all over me!" All of those calculate to the same thing: *"I can't!"*

There was a rabbit stuck in a hole. He yelled and yelled for someone to help him get unstuck. A frog hopped along and asked, "What's wrong?" The rabbit said, "I'm stuck! I have wiggled and squirmed and pushed, but I can't get out. I just can't. Will you get a ladder and help me get free?" The frog exhausted himself dragging a ladder back to the rabbit's hole. When he was almost there, he saw the rabbit standing outside the hole. The frog dropped the ladder angrily, hopped over to the rabbit, and said, "I thought you said you couldn't get out of your hole!" The rabbit explained apologetically, *"I couldn't,* but a snake crawled in the other end and *I did!"*

Don't say "I can't!" when you really mean "I won't!" You can if you want to!

CHAPTER 12
Facing Your Failures

Being at the wrong place at the right time and being at the right place at the wrong time are forms of failure. All of us blow it continually, but we would rather cover up our failures as if they weren't there. Or we would like to sow wild oats all week and then on Sunday pray for a crop failure! We also find it much easier to openly discuss the failure in others. It's said that the church's favorite indoor sport is confessing the sins of others.

Some preachers today teach that God would have us all be healthy, wealthy, and basically perfect. They would have us believe that there is an endless supply of miracles waiting to be claimed to protect us from failure.

Instead of facing our failures and dealing with them, many of us are spending most of our time waiting on miracles!

WHY SO MUCH FAILURE?
The Devil Made Me Do It!

God created the world, including man, and set in motion the principles of life that make life work. Because of the cultish tendency of various forms of religion (Christianity included), these principles have been turned into ugly, boxy regulations. God's positive principles that make life work best have been marketed as negative, narrow rules that stifle man's freedom.

The Biblical concept of failure is wrapped up in the term *sin*. Sin is a self-centered rebellion against

God's principles and standards. It all started in the original family in the garden. The Devil, President of Evil, Inc., tempted Eve to rebel and eat the "apricot" so she could experience "true life." She ate it and lured Adam into the same rebellion. They both ate, and both found out that by rebelling against God's way they began to experience death rather than the promised "true life."

God is not the author of evil. The credit goes to the President of Evil, Inc.! God allowed freedom within his creation to choose obedience or disobedience. That freedom is called humanity.

Be Careful of Falling Short

Today men and women are irreversibly caught up in this same self-centered rebellion against God's principles and standards. Because of the original failure of man and woman, we are unable to do anything but fall short of God's standards. Another definition of sin is missing the mark or falling short. We are all by nature sinful before God. This includes such sins as lying (from gross lies to the little white ones), murder (including hating another person), and adultery (lusting after another person's mate).

The scorpion asked the turtle for a ride across the lake. The turtle argued, "I'm afraid that you would sting me when we got halfway across!" The scorpion said, "Are you crazy? If I did that, we would both drown!" The turtle agreed, the scorpion climbed on his back, and away they went. About halfway across the lake, the scorpion stung the turtle. As they were going under the turtle said, "You fool, why did you do this? You're going to drown with me!" The scorpion responded, "I don't know.

It's just my nature!'' In the same way, we are by
nature sinful.

WHAT IS GOD'S ATTITUDE
TOWARD FAILURE?
The Principle of Retribution
According to the first chapter of Romans, two
principles are in effect in our world. The first is the
principle of retribution. This principle is the unfolding of man's sin and failure. The principle of
retribution says that when you sin (rebel against or
fall short of God's principles and standards), you
pay. There is a price tag for this failure. You talk
about stress! This is megastress! Look at this:

> For the wrath of God [the principle of
> retribution] is revealed from heaven against all
> ungodliness and unrighteousness of men, who
> suppress the truth in unrighteousness,
> because that which is known about God is evi-
> dent within them. For since the creation of the
> world His invisible attributes, His eternal
> power and divine nature, have been clearly
> seen, being understood through what has been
> made, so that they are without excuse. For
> even though they knew God, they did not
> honor Him as God, or give thanks; but they
> became futile in their speculations, and their
> foolish heart was darkened. Professing to be
> wise, they became fools, and exchanged the
> glory of the incorruptible God for an image in
> the form of corruptible man and of birds and
> four-footed animals and crawling creatures.
> Therefore God gave them over in the lusts of
> their hearts to impurity, that their bodies
> might be dishonored among them. For they ex-

changed the truth of God for a lie, and worshiped and served the creature rather than the Creator, who is blessed forever. Amen. For this reason God gave them over to degrading passions; for their women exchanged the natural function for that which is unnatural, and in the same way also the men abandoned the natural function of the woman and burned in their desire toward one another, men with men committing indecent acts and receiving in their own persons the due penalty of their error. And just as they did not see fit to acknowledge God any longer, God gave them over to a depraved mind, to do those things which are not proper, being filled with all unrighteousness, wickedness, greed, evil; full of envy, murder, strife, deceit, malice; they are gossips, slanderers, haters of God, insolent, arrogant, boastful, inventors of evil, disobedient to parents, without understanding, untrustworthy, unloving, unmerciful; and, although they know the ordinance of God, that those who practice such things are worthy of death, they not only do the same, but also give hearty approval to those who practice them (Romans 1:18-32).

The Principle of Righteousness

The second basic principle in effect, according to Romans 1, is the *principle of righteousness.* This principle is the unfolding of God's program to save man from his own sin and failure. The principle of retribution describes man's grossness, but the principle of righteousness distributes God's grace to all who need it. Grace is the undeserved forgiveness and favor of God to man.

God has set up the principles and standards for living, and at the same time He offers the power for us to be forgiven—even reinstated in a positive relationship with Him. The most incredible thing about the principle of righteousness is that it offers the only power of reversal for man's failure. As a matter of fact, man's sin and failure even trigger the grace of God. Whenever I sin, God orders another bucket of grace to pour over my failure. Sometimes I need a whole bathtub full of grace! It's the great reversal *from gross to grace, from enslavement to freedom, from death to life, and from paying for your sin to having it paid for.*

Let's look at the principle of righteousness—grace:

For I am not ashamed of the gospel, for it is the power of God for salvation to everyone who believes, to the Jew first and also to the Greek. For in it the righteousness of God [the principle of righteousness] is revealed from faith to faith; as it is written, "BUT THE RIGHTEOUS MAN SHALL LIVE BY FAITH" (Romans 1:16,17).

WHAT ARE WE TO DO WITH FAILURE?

There's some good news about failure. In light of man's grossness and God's grace, the good news is what man must do to personally apply this grace. There is an initial application and then a continuous flow of grace. Both require the same action—*facing your failures!*

The initial application of the good news of grace requires that you acknowledge your sin (failures), that you cannot pay for it on your own, and that you accept God's grace (forgiveness) for your sin. All of this is wrapped up in believing in Jesus, God's Son. Jesus Himself articulated it in this way:

For God so loved the world that He gave His

only begotten Son, that whoever believes in Him should not perish, but have eternal life. For God did not send His Son into the world to judge the world, but that the world should be saved through Him. He who believes in Him is not judged; he who does not believe has been judged already, because he has not believed in the name of the only begotten Son of God. And this is the judgment, that the light is come into the world, and men loved the darkness rather than the light; for their deeds were evil. For everyone who does evil hates the light, and does not come to the light, lest his deeds should be exposed. But he who practices the truth comes to the light, that his deeds may be manifested as having been wrought in God. . . . He who believes in the Son has eternal life; but he who does not obey the Son shall not see life, but the wrath of God abides on him" (John 3:16-21, 36).

The *continuous application of the good news of grace* also requires that you face your failures. Can you imagine the energy expended trying to cover up, blame, deny, or ignore failures? The price tag is enormous for that stress overload!

The amazing thing to me is that people who have initially applied God's grace are the biggest offenders of its continuous power! These are the people who are attempting to play the "perfection game"—not admitting their failures. In a real sense they are X-ing God out of their lives. And when God is missing, there is no relief of stress and no hope of reversal from gross to grace.

Facing your failures in this continuous application of God's grace is twofold. It's summed up in this verse:

> If we confess our sins [failures], He is faithful and righteous to forgive us our sins and to cleans us from all unrighteousness (1 John 1:9).

First, in facing your failures *you must* register *your confession.* Confession is literally "agreeing with." Registering your confession is simply to agree with God about your failures—that you have a self-centered rebellion or have fallen short of God's principles and standards. A clergyman, tears, or other people are unnecessary to register your confession.

Second, in facing your failures as you register your confession, *God releases your cleansing.* Your confession triggers the buckets and bathtubs of grace in order to cleanse your life. We get so clogged up with guilt, fears, and anxieties and are in need of a cleanup! There is nothing more needful today than spiritual and psychological cleansing. And I've seen *nothing* to clean people *better* (not simply reform them, but really cleanse them) than God's cleaning service! *Face your failures by registering your confession and releasing your cleansing.*

Almost everyone had given up on two delinquent kids. Nothing seemed to work in turning them around. Then someone had the bright idea of taking them before Father Harrigan, a tough priest across town.

Father Harrigan bellowed out, "Where is God?" The kid was so shocked that he didn't know what to say. Again the priest forcefully said, "Where is God? Tell me right now! Where is God?" The force of the priest made the frightened kid clam up completely.

Father Harrigan dismissed the first kid to the waiting room with instructions to send his friend in. The waiting delinquent asked, "What happened in there, man?" His buddy said, "Well, apparently God is missing and they're trying to pin that on us too!"

When God is missing, it's impossible to face your failures successfully!

CHAPTER 13
*Living Life on Purpose**

Have you ever felt like Humpty Dumpty—pushed and pressured to pieces?

Unlike Humpty Dumpty, who even with the help of all the king's horses and all the king's men couldn't get himself back together again, most people can get themselves back together again. But they climb back on their walls, only to be pushed off all over again! After a few more pushes knock you off precarious walls, you discover that it becomes increasingly more difficult to pull yourself together again. But why so many falls off so many walls? It's your perspective—or your lack of it!

A full perspective forces you to ask pertinent questions about your pleasures (sitting on walls) and your predicaments (falling off walls). Why do I like sitting on walls? Who pushed me? Why was I pushed? Why do I fall when I'm pushed? Why do I break into pieces when I fall? Why do I feel I've lost another piece every time I try to put myself back together again? As you begin to answer these perspective questions you are launched into a new lifestyle—that of knowing about yourself and taking control of what you know. You can then begin to act rather than react—to live life by your choice rather than by your circumstances or choice of other people.

*Portions of this chapter are adapted from Tim Timmons, *Maximum Living in a Pressure-cooker World* (Waco, Texas: Word Books, 1979), Chapter 1. Used by permission.

Most people are suffering from a faulty perspective. There are at least three types of faulty perspectives. The first is a passive perspective. Here you may understand all there is to know about walls, pushes, and falls, and even be committed to what you know, but you aren't personally involved in your commitment. In other words, you are committed to what you should do theoretically, but you aren't practicing it. You aren't following through. You're like the kamikaze pilot who flew 33 missions!

The second type of faulty perspective is a partial perspective. Here you have a limited knowledge about walls, pushes, and falls. You just do not see the whole picture, and consequently you lack an adequate basis for action. I experience this constantly when I counsel with couples. Almost every time I see the husband and wife separately, I get a faulty perspective on their marital situation. After I've listened to the wife, I'm convinced she's married to the number one clod of the year. Then her husband walks in, and as I listen to his side of the story I become convinced he should be given a medal for hanging in there! Until I can move to a fuller perspective, my partial perspective paralyzes me from acting wisely.

The third type of faulty perspective is a prejudiced perspective. Through this perspective lens you view the walls, pushes, and falls the way you want to view them, in spite of every evidence to the contrary. Many people absolutely refuse to acknowledge evidence, as the following scenario so clearly and cleverly illustrates.

Once upon a time there was a man who thought he was dead. His concerned wife and friends sent him to the friendly neighborhood psychiatrist. The psychiatrist determined to cure him by convincing him of one fact that contradicted his belief that he was dead. The psychiatrist decided to use the simple truth that dead men to not bleed. He put his patient to work reading medical texts, observing autopsies, and so on. After weeks of effort the patient finally said, "All right, all right! You've convinced me! Dead men do not bleed." Whereupon the psychiatrist stuck him in the arm with a needle, and blood flowed. The man who thought he was dead looked down with a contorted, ashen face and cried out, "Good Lord! Dead men do bleed after all!"

Since a faulty perspective—passive or partial or prejudiced—is so common, then how do you cultivate a full and balanced perspective on life's pleasures and predicaments? The answer is simple, yet surprising. *Think!*

It's estimated that only 5 percent of the world think, 15 percent think they think, and 80 percent would rather die than think! An educational study showed that when people are presented with a new concept, 50 percent go along with it and 30 percent don't, both without thinking or evaluating, 15 percent take longer to make a decision but still without thinking or evaluating, and 5 percent truly think and evaluate before making a decision.

Sales industries consistently find that approximately 5 percent of their salespeople rise to the top and are responsible for the majority of their productivity. It's also interesting to note that when faced with sickness, a tragedy, or a crisis of some sort, only 5 percent will come through it all a better person. The other 95 percent will come out worse for the experience!

A 5 percenter—a thinker! Thinking is the process

of expanding your perspective on life. It's the art of viewing the whole wall without finding yourself in midair. As you expand your perspective, you may discover that you have several (not just one) options as to where you sit (not on walls) or stand. You may also discover that you don't want to sit on walls anymore!

With a faulty perspective, life (people and circumstances) controls you, but with a full perspective you can take control of life. Instead of feeling like Humpty Dumpty, always getting pushed and pressured to pieces, you can make things happen on purpose—positive things. Living life on purpose will help you live life with more *confidence* in yourself, *compassion* for others, and *commitment* to the future.

Plugging into Life

We are overstressed much of the time because we are living the life of a ping-pong ball—bouncing from one table surface to another and knocked about from paddle to paddle! A very critical action step in processing the pressure is to *live life on purpose.* It's living with a plan or strategy to make life really work.

Alan Lakein, an authority on time management, believes that we waste 80 percent of our time even though we are perpetually busy. The problem comes because we don't know what to do with our lives and we don't know how to reach our goals. We're not even sure of our goals anymore! Worse than anything else, we just don't know how to plug into life.[1]

LIFE TRACKS FOR PEOPLE

Just as a train functions most freely on its two

tracks, so a person functions most freely and effectively on three life tracks. In fact, these three tracks are evident everywhere in humanity, both within the psyche of a person and within personal relationships. I've observed the dynamics of these life tracks in counseling and in every form of communication. These life tracks motivate people into action and are also necessary for psychological wellness. *When a person is off the track in any of these areas he is psychologically sick.*

Life Track of Responsibility

The life track of responsibility is the need to be doing something worthwhile in this world. It's important to know that your life counts for something. This is usually experienced through vocation or community involvements.

Modern man easily becomes subject to technology and mass impersonalization. Rather than being free and creative and able to take advantage of a higher technology, he becomes less than a zero. The principle of success has become so important that anything which leads to it is considered morally right. But this twists man and denies his essential humanity. If you strive for success at the cost of being human, what have you gained? When the job is more important than the healthy humanity of the worker, our society is sick. It's a wind up society.[2]

Only in creative activity do you externalize the unique identity you have as a person. What distinguishes you from an animal is the possibility of being creative beyond the immediate environment. You can alter and enlarge your world, but the porpoise can't. The life track of responsibility requires that you feel good about achievement and accomplishment, and if you don't you become derailed off this important life track! This is the beginning of psychological illness.[3]

If you feel yourself becoming derailed, do something about it. If you're dissatisfied with your job, change what can be changed within the job, or else change the job. If you cannot find the sense of doing something worthwhile in your job, make some worthwhile commitments to be involved in church or community groups. In other words, if you are derailed, fix it before you fall apart at the seams. To be derailed here causes a sense of depreciation.

Life Track of Reality

The life track of reality is the need to have a solid base for living—a foundation for right and wrong. It's a full awareness of strengths and weaknesses— a full knowledge of who and why you are.

This life track answers the question, "Why are you alive?" To stay alive only for a job or another person is not enough. This life track is at the very core of your existence. This is where your relationship with God and His principles belongs. Without this God-consciousness there is nothing but a vacuum. People stuff all kinds of things into this vacuum—money, sex, business, cars, family, church, etc. But nothing fits except God Himself! To be derailed off this life track is to live in a constant state of dissatisfaction.

Life Track Relationships

The life track of relationships is the need to be well-connected with people. It's important to enjoy a healthy context of relationships—family and extended family. The need to be interrelated and interdependent is a major factor in the reduction of stress overload.

To be derailed from this life track is even more serious than the first or second derailment. Derailment off the life track of relationships will affect the other two tracks in a negative way. In order to carry out your *responsibilities* or to fully experience *reality*, your relationships must be on track. Off the track the person's entire life can be derailed by the poor or bad relationships. This derailment causes a cold sense of detachment in a crowded world.

Each of these life tracks is critical for dissolving stress in your family. To be derailed in any one or combination of these life tracks is to be emotionally sick. If completely derailed, a slow death as a person is certain. I've talked with many people who have already died but aren't buried yet! The psychological wreckage is everywhere, and the only way to survive this wreckage is to live life on purpose.

CHAPTER 14
Victim or Victor?

In a flight from New York to New Orleans the engines began to sputter and then one by one went out. The pilot radioed back, "Ladies and gentlemen, all our engines except one have gone out and we're quickly losing altitude. But don't worry, I'm going for help!"

Have you ever felt as helpless as those passengers? When your back's against the wall, what do you do? When you've done all you can do and still the pressure is turned on "High," what else can be done? No matter the trial, you can become the victor and not the victim!

There are three principles and three promises in the spiritual realm that offer hope to anyone whose back is against the wall but who has a relationship with God. It's not a spiritual cop-out, but a principle of life that has overwhelming results. According to James 1, these principles are:

1. **Refocus on the Product**
   James says:
   Consider it all joy, my brethren, when you encounter various trials, knowing that the testing of your faith produces endurance. And let endurance have its perfect result, that you may be perfect and complete, lacking in nothing (James 1:2-4).
   When your back is against the wall with trials and pressures, first *refocus on the product!* The natural thing to do is to focus on the trials. But the principle of life says to focus on the product. What

will you learn or gain through this stressful trial? You will gain endurance or perseverance in order to live through new trials. You may gain a new compassion and insight to help others going through a similar trial. Whatever the trial thrown up at you, find the handle to it. Look for the positive side—the product. Refocus on the product!

The promise associated with this principle is in Romans 8:

> And we know that God causes all things to work together for good to those who love God (Romans 8:28).

God promises to work all things together for good to those who love Him. He doesn't promise to work it out so that the bad thing that happened is made good. But He promises to work this bad trial *together* with something to produce good for you! Trials are not good, nor will God make them good. A death of a loved one is not good, but He will work it together with something else for some good to come out of it! What a terrific promise!

2. Request His Power

James says:

> But if any of you lacks wisdom, let him ask of God, who gives to all men generously and without reproach, and it will be given to him. But let him ask in faith without any doubting, for the one who doubts is like the surf of the sea driven and tossed by the wind. For let not that man expect that he will receive anything from the Lord, being a double-minded man, unstable in all his ways (James 1:5-8).

When your back is against the wall with stressful trials, *request His power*—specifically His wisdom.

At a desperate time like this you need supernatural wisdom to know what to do. James warns us not to ask for wisdom with a doubting attitude, because God is willing to give His wisdom to anyone who asks. Believe Him!

The specific promise connected with this principle is in 1 Corinthians 10:

No temptation [trial] has overtaken you but such as is common to man; and God is faithful, who will not allow you to be tempted beyond what you are able, but with the temptation will provide the way of escape also, that you may be able to endure it (1 Corinthians 10:13).

Here God promises that no matter how overwhelming the stressful trials may be, He will provide a way of escape so that you can endure them. The picture is that of a great mountain of trials, with the "escape" being a mountain pass promised so that the great mountain can be crossed. You can count on God's promise that the mountain pass will be provided *in the midst of* your stressful trials!

3. **Reconsider Your Position**

James continues:

But let the brother of humble circumstances glory in his high position; and let the rich man glory in his humiliation, because like flowering grass he will pass away. For the sun rises with a scorching wind, and withers the grass; and its flower falls off, and the beauty of its appearance is destroyed; so too the rich man in the midst of his pursuits will fade away (James 1:9-11).

When your back is against the wall with stressful trials, *reconsider your position.* It's not your earthly position, but your heavenly position before God that is to be considered. You see, your position with your Creator is all that really matters when your back is against the wall. The greater the stress, the easier it is to reconsider what really matters. As people face the tragedy of terminal disease, I've never encountered one person who was not most concerned about his standing before God.

He challenges the rich and the poor alike. The rich man is to reconsider the fact that all those material riches don't count for much before God. You came into this world barefoot all over and will exit the same way! The poor man is to glory in the fact that his low material status on earth isn't all there is. He is to glory in his high spiritual status before God. In other words, each man is to reconsider his position before God and count it as most important in stressful times.

The promise associated with the principle is in Philippians 1:

> For I am confident of this very thing, that He who began a good work in you will perfect it until the day of Christ Jesus (Philippians 1:6).

God promises to continue His work in you for your entire life! In other words, your initial application of God's grace to your life was not a cheap, temporary, religious experience, but a long-term growth dynamic completely empowered by God's work.

Go Positive on God!

All three principles and promises demonstrate how to be a victor rather than a victim. Victims focus on their problems, which normally inflates the molehill problems into impossible mountains.

They spend all their energies going negative on the problem and even enjoy talking about it rather than doing anything about it.

When your back is against the wall because of stressful trials, don't go negative on the problem. Go positive on God—refocus on the product, request His power, and reconsider your position. Going positive on God is taking Him at His word and counting on His promises! So thank and praise God for His product, power, and position that He provides you in the midst of your stressful trials.

A bird in the barnyard was about to freeze to death. A man walking through the barnyard noticed the bird's dilemma and wrapped it up in a fresh pile of manure. The bird was warmed in his new environment and began to sing loudly. Another man heard the bird singing away and assumed it was stuck. So he unwrapped the bird and set it free. Within a couple of hours the bird froze to death!

There are three morals to this story:

1. It's not always your enemy who gets you into a mess.

2. It's not always your friend who gets you out.

3. If you find yourself in a mess up to your neck, for goodness sake don't sing about it!

When your back is against the wall, don't go negative on the problem and sing about it. Go positive on God! You'll be the victor!

CHAPTER 15
*Mind Your Own Life**

Decisions! Choices! Commitments! Life is a series of responsibilities (which demand decisions, choices, and commitments) lived out in the context of relationships. Every day we are faced with choices. At the same time we have become experts at avoiding those choices and responsibilities.

Some people are very decisive, but only when it comes to avoiding decisions!

Two major decisions must be made in order to *mind your own life*. First, a physical decision is necessary with respect to what you do with your "load." Second, a psychological decision is necessary with respect to what you do with the resident of your body.

PHYSICAL DECISION
You Are What You Eat?

Among the numerous changes brought about by civilization within the modern era, none is more profound or of greater importance than that in the realm of man's diet. Many of these changes have been good and even necessary due to the large concentration of people in cities. But unfortunately, many of these changes have been detrimental to the health of man and no doubt account for many of the illnesses that are associated with modern living. Within the area of diet and nutrition so much

*Portions of this chapter are adapted from Tim Timmons, *Loneliness Is Not a Disease* (Harvest House, 1981), Chapter 6.

misinformation is dispensed that it's difficult for anyone to know the truth. There are natural laws which govern diet and nutrition, just as natural laws govern everything else in nature. Man is a creature of natural law, and he must follow it. The penalty for disobeying the laws of nature are poor health, degenerative diseases, and eventual extinction. This violation causes great stress in the family.[1]

You Are What You Digest

There is in existence a facet of diet and eating that is of extreme importance to anyone endeavoring to eat properly and maintain health that is virutally unknown in the medical-health establishment. It's proper food combining! If you were to properly combine your foods, and not do another thing toward losing weight, you would feel lighter and increase your health. It's a subject of utmost importance, but doctors never even mention to you the importance of adhering to some basic rules of food combining.[2]

The digestive enzymes of the human digestive tract have certain well-defined limitations, and when you eat in such a manner as to overtax these limitations, you run into digestive difficulties. Proper food combining is merely a sane way of respecting your enzymic limitations. If you will combine your food properly and not eat them haphazardly and indiscriminately, you will assure yourself better and more-efficient digestion. Benefits you receive from the more-efficient operation of your digestive system are many. The nerve energy you save by not overworking your digestive system can be used in breaking down and eliminating the excess that you have built up over the years through negligent eating habits.[3]

No other animal in nature has the great variety of different foods spread before him at a meal that civilized people have. Certainly a meat-eating animal would not have bread or potatoes with its meat. Deer grazing in the forest combine their food very little. Squirrels eating nuts eat their fill of nuts and take no other food with them. Birds have been observed to eat insects at one time of day, seeds at another. Humans, on the other hand, have been known to attack an incredibly diversified array of different foods at one time and are also the only "animal" to develop such a diversified array of different maladies![4]

Conventional eating habits violate all the rules of proper food combining. People will deny that the condemned combinations that they always eat can hurt them, but health and disease are not an accident. It is a proven fact that a change to correctly combine meals is followed by an immediate improvement in health as a consequence of the lighter load the digestive organs have to carry. By assuming better digestion, nutrition is improved and there is less gas in the system to deal with. The better food is digested, the more nutrition you receive, and these nutriments are the builders of nerve energy. As a result you not only *feel* lighter, but your body, unhindered by excess gases and the work it has to do to eliminate them, concentrates on the shedding of the toxicity and extra weight you are carrying around.[5]

There are basically three different types of foods: protein, carbohydrates, and sugars. All three require different digestive juices in the system, and none work at optimum level when forced to work in conjunction with one another. In fact, in many cases when one interacts with another, both are neutralized. The simpler you can make your meals by not eating too many mixtures at one time, the less work your digestive tract will have to perform, thereby conserving more energy that can be put to better use elsewhere.[6]

The entire function is complicated when you start discussing all the different interactions. It's too complicated to delve into deeply. Basically, there are several stages of digestion, and if the preceding stage is not properly performed, the following one is thwarted or at best interfered with. By not combining correctly, the food spoils inside your digestive tract. This not only wastes the food, but even worse, it results in the production of gases and toxins in your system.[7]

You live on three types of basic raw materials: *carbohydrates, fats, and proteins.* Nutritionists agree with these basics, but vehemently disagree with one another as to the amounts and varying combinations that are most healthful.

Let me add my own opinion to the myriad of opinions already out there! After extensive personal study as a layman, I'm convinced that *you are not what you eat! You are what you digest!* The following is not a plan for perfect nutrition, but a plan for raising your level of health. We have been using it and have found it to be a low-stress, nutritional strategy for maximum health.

Principle 1: *Avoid* refined white flour, sugar, and chemicals.

Principle 2: *Consume* as much as you want of natural and living foods. This includes vegetables, fruits, and nuts.

Principle 3: *Reduce* your meat intake, especially the red meats. Limit your meat to once per day for lunch or dinner or eliminate meat altogether on some days.

Principle 4: The high protein-low carbohydrate diet is a bad rumor! Combine your foods carefully.

1. Eat nothing but fruit all morning.

2. Have a salad every day.

3. Be careful of combining two or more concentrated foods such as meat, potatoes, rice, dairy products, and breads. (If you combine, it will be a real gasser!)

Principle 5: *Cleanse* your body of its poisonous toxins by a 24-36 hour fast with only juice or water, or have a fruit-only day. (Fasting or fruiting one day per week is very healthful.)

Run For Your Life

To *think* your best, to *feel* your best, and to be able to *do* your best, you must move! A regular exercise plan is necessary to raise your health level and to reduce your stress level.

The best kind of exercise is that which helps your heart and circulation. It involves moving your arms and, more importantly, your legs. Any exercise that makes you breathe heavily and break into a sweat is a good one. It's recommended that the best exercise must last for 30-60 minutes at least four times per week.

Many sports or exercises do not qualify as an adequate exertion on the body to produce any healthful results. This is illustrated by the fact that some athletes seem to live long, while others don't live even as long as the average man or woman. There seems to be an interesting correlation between the types of physical activity and the longe-

vity of the athlete. In a study of the lifespans of athletes listed in *Who's Who in American Sports*, it was found that:
   —Football players died at a mean age of 57.
   —Boxers died at a mean age of 61.
   —Baseball players died at a mean age of 64.
   —Track runners died at a mean age of 71.
Only 65 percent of the football players lived more than 50 years, compared with 87 percent of the runners. Why? It might be because running is a sustained, long-muscle, dynamic exercise. The others are stop-and-go, with substantial periods of layoffs and nonexercise.[8]

I am hooked on running. It helps my body to function on all cylinders and my mind to think more clearly, and it greatly reduces my constant stress overload. When I don't run, I can tell it. In fact, when I don't run, I'm a little on-edge and uptight (not easy to live with). Ask my wife—she can tell the difference!

I am also a crusader for exercise. Instead of giving my pitch, let me suggest a beginning program that fits anybody's body and lifestyle. It's found in a book: *Aerobics,* by Kenneth H. Cooper. Remember, when your body is stressed, it demands some action. So get your act together and start exercising!

Your physical decision? *Eat right and exercise regularly!*

PSYCHOLOGICAL DECISION

The psychological decision that must be made is regarding your body's resident—you! The greatest stress on your life and family is brought about by the lack of relationship—loneliness! So a decision is necessary in order to counteract this greatest personal and family stressor of all.

The Mental Connection

Until the late nineteenth century, most people did not believe that they were responsible for their own physical health, a belief that has lingered on into the late twentieth century. Even today, many people resist the idea that there is a connection between their loneliness and their health. They will believe that human disease is caused by germs "out there" and that nothing they do matters.[9]

Psychologically, the exact same avoidance is used. People find much comfort in labeling their problems as allergies and diseases or blaming their parents and life circumstances. Even in Christianity, instead of personal responsibility the "spiritual" thing is to be "led by God." The incredible thing is that God seems to "lead" people to do the strangest, most unethical, irresponsible things. That which is responsible is always outside of ourselves—"out there."

Psychosis (mental disorientation—acting crazy) is rarely understood as a choice by either the adult who adopts it or by the people who are involved with him: his doctor, family, employer, or friends. If any people involved with him suspect that the psychosis is indeed a choice, they find it difficult to say so. Voicing such a suspicion makes everyone uncomfortable because everyone then has or might believe he has some responsibility for not relieving the loneliness that caused the patient to choose psychosis. It is much easier for everyone to believe that the person just got "sick" and that no one has any responsibility for what happened.

In addition, we do not like to admit that craziness is a choice, because we are all a little crazy at times; if we admit that it is a choice for others, we must also admit that it is a choice for ourselves. The patient who will not admit he had made a choice because he would then see that both his previous lonely life and his present crazy life are self-created. His symptoms are of course specifically chosen to help him avoid such an understanding. The doctor will not admit it is a choice because he would then have to admit that mental illness as a disease is only a scientific fantasy. Such an admission would conflict with his omnipotent healing role: a doctor cannot heal craziness as he can appendicitis or streptococcus sore throat.[10]

Traditional counseling avoids action in the present by delving into the past to discover when the patient first experienced failure and loneliness. It is important to understand why you feel the way you feel and how past experiences have affected you. But much of the time a search into the past is harmful because it almost always becomes an end in itself, an intellectual involvement that precludes the lonely person from doing *now* what he should be doing in the real world—*learning to become successfully involved with others.*

It is wrong to avoid the issue of present behavior by searching for remote periods of loneliness or for rejections early in life when the symptom was learned. The wrong is compounded by excusing a patient's lonely, incompetent involvement with his symptom by labeling the symptom an illness. *Three errors—encouraging the patient to blot out the present, excusing the patient's involvement with the symptom, and labeling his symptom as an illness—relieve the patient from the responsibility of learning successful involvement with others, of facing his loneliness and failure, and of admitting that his symptom is his own choice.*[11]

KNOCKED AROUND BY LIFE

The reason that many of us never even begin to break away from the grip of loneliness is that we insist on making other people responsible for our individual fears of love and intimacy. This was natural when we were helpless, dependent little people. But in playing the role of victims beyond childhood it is possible to go through life merely *reacting* to other people and events, and never assuming personal responsibility for *acting. Where that is the case, loneliness is of our own doing.*[12] Victimizing ourselves into reactionaries is like volunteering to be a ping-pong ball—knocked around by anyone who wants to play!

The loneliest people are those who have decided to stop loving. It's a choice! It is of our own doing. We may sometimes say that we have good reasons for doing so. But whenever we do, it is because we have allowed ourselves to be hurt to the point *where we actually believe* "it's all their fault." *Victims always feel lonely.* As long as we keep justifying or defending our position, there is no hope of breaking free from the shackles of loneliness.[13]

As victims we are unwilling to take the responsibility for our *decisions, feelings,* and *behavior.* The prospect is frightening. We are forever mumbling, "If it weren't for them . . . you . . . her . . . him." But behind this theme song there is a fear of accepting personal responsibility for our *decisions.* We always turn sour. We are not willing to give a firm and resounding yes or no to anything or anyone. Characterized by such halfhearted statements as "I'll try," "maybe," "I suppose," and "I hope so," we will do anything to avoid having to make a definite commitment.[14]

There Is Hope!

If loneliness were a disease savagely attacking human beings everywhere, then there is little hope for a soon discovery of its cure. But *loneliness is not a disease. It's a decision! It's a decision to avoid the fears of the pain accompanying identity* (companion pain of dissatisfaction), *inadequacy* (companion pain of depreciation), and *intimacy* (companion of detachment). *Since loneliness is a decision and not a disease, there is hope!* If a decision or series of decisions can relieve my loneliness, then inside loneliness is hope.

Loneliness and Love

Man is essentially alone and lonely, and from this isolation he cannot be saved by someone else but only by himself through the fact that he loves. It is *the fear of love which is the root cause of every attitude and forum of behavior that separates us from each other.* The most telling sign of our personness—our fear—is difficult to detect, even feel sometimes, because it is not always characterized by a sudden onset of trembling, sweating palms, or knots in the stomach. Since it is a root condition of life, it is an inherent component of our personhood.[15]

We are lonely because of our fear of love. The fear of love is the foundational fear which underlies the fear of identity (the love of who you are), the fear of inadequacy (the love of what you do), and the fear of intimacy (the love of others).

Loneliness and love go hand in hand. To be aware of love, in its real sense, is loneliness: the hopes, the joys, the ecstasy, all the tensions of loss and fulfillment of dreams and despair. Loneliness is an inevitable outcome of real love, but it is also a process through which new love becomes possible. Love has no meaning without loneliness; loneliness is the other side of love. *Just as people decide to be lonely, so must there be a decision to love!*[16]

Finding the Lost Self

Our greatest mistake is in not distinguishing between "being alone" and "loneliness." Our periods of being alone, if simply allowed to be experienced by ourselves, can be among the most rewarding of our lives. It *is* possible to be alone and not be lonely.[17] But let's look again at Erich Fromm's comments about being alone: "We have developed a phobia of being alone; we prefer the utmost trivial and even obnoxious company, the most meaningless activities, to being alone with ourselves; we seem to be frightened at the prospect of facing ourselves. Is it because we feel we would be such bad company? (Erich Fromm, *Man for Himself*). We need to face ourselves so desperately, but we fear it so much! At the innermost core of all loneliness is a deep and powerful yearning for union—an appointment with one's lost self.

The saying "If you can't make it with people you can't make it" has a corrollary: "If you can only make it with people, and not alone, you can't make it."[18] Being alone has a quality of immediacy and depth; it is a significant experience—one of the few in modern life in which man communes with himself. And in such communion man comes to grips with his own being. He discovers life, who he is, what he really wants, the meaning of his existence, and the true nature of his relations with other people. He may see and realize for the first time truths which have been obscured for a long time. Distortions suddenly become naked and transparent.[19]

It is in this state of naked isolation that the potential for growth and change exist. Being alone is an important place to make an appointment with yourself.

But if your experiences of being alone are not by appointment, but come from the flow of natural events, over which you have no control, there are two options: 1. in not allowing yourself to accept them the separation can defeat you and leave you in a state of unresolved despair for the rest of your life because you decide that you will never risk loving again; 2. allowing yourself to accept being alone can serve ultimately to bring out the best possibilities. It can give you the time to examine who you are and what you want, to evaluate your goals and the quality of your work, and to appreciate your husband or wife, your friends, or even God.[20]

Conquering the Fear of Love

A psychiatrist was asked, "How can you teach people to love?" He answered the question by a couple of his own: "Have you ever had a toothache?" He made his point. When we are in pain, even if it is only the passing discomfort of a toothache, we are thinking about ourselves.

The psychiatrist continued, "This is a pain-filled world in which we are living. And the pains that reside deep in the human hearts around us are not like toothaches. We go to bed at night with them and we wake up with them in the morning . . . . This is a pain-filled world, and so a loveless world that we live in. Most human beings are so turned-in by their own pains that they cannot get enough out of themselves to love to any great extent."[21]

Loneliness is a decision based upon the fear of love, and therefore a decision to love and be loved is critical in relieving loneliness. But a decision alone is not enough. You must decide to do something. Learn to mind your own life—physically and psychologically!

CHAPTER 16
Women Are Weird and Men Are Strange

In 1970, 96 percent of all Americans declared themselves dedicated to the ideal of two people sharing a life and a home together. A decade later the number was precisely the same—a virtually universal 96 percent. Why then do we experience the battle of the sexes at every level of society?[1]

I'm convinced that the battle lingers on because we continually violate the most basic principle of the sexes—difference! We strive for equality (which is desirable) and achieve sameness (which is destructive). But men and women are incurably different. And it's only when we understand that difference that we are free to be complementary to each other.

When not demonstrating for equality, we carefully put our masks in place and play the roles that have gradually become comfortable. Roles may be comfortable, but they are not for real. When people play their roles they don't relate. On the contrary, playing roles turns a relationship into empty ritual and cold routine. Disappointed by this hollow shell of a relationship, people desperately search for another one. They hope *this* one will work. In most cases, this new venture slips into the need for *new* roles with new masks to play a different game. But 96 percent of us keep trying to make it work!

The only possible way to defuse this great sexual war is to sharpen the focus on the complementary difference between men and women. I'm a firm believer that women are weird and men are very strange!

DO YOU LOVE ME?

A woman will ask her man, "Do you love me?" (It's 8:00). "Are you sure?" (8:10) "You really do?" (8:15) "You do, huh?" (8:20). In the meantime her man is thinking (and perhaps saying), "I told you I loved you when we were married. And it's still in effect until I revoke it!" Now that's a big difference in outlook!

That same kind of difference is illustrated when a couple receives an invitation to a party. The woman's response is, "What shall I wear?" and the man's, "How can I get out of this?"

IN THE NOW OR OUT THERE SOMEWHERE?

Most women initially respond in the immediate—*in the now.* She is rarely "out there," but lives right here in the now. Most men initially respond in long-range manner. He is rarely *here*, but lives *out there somewhere.*

Years ago I came home enthusiastically announcing that we were going to the Middle East for a short tour. Carol's response was like a wet blanket on my excitement. I was looking forward to this trip eight months in the future and she asked me four piddly questions in the *now!* They were: How can we afford it? Who will keep the kids? What will we do with the house? What about the car? All my enthusiasm was quickly dampened.

But it wasn't her fault! She was simply acting characteristically as a woman. I should have realized that she was viewing this situation in the now. My mistake was to ignore the *now.* I could have approached it in this way: "Honey, I have a topic sentence and a few things to follow. Topic sentence: We're going to the Middle East. *Hold it!*

It's paid for. I know who will keep the kids. I believe we'll leave the house right here, and we'll put the car in the garage." Now I have met her need of the immediate and freed her up to get excited about the long-range future.

The flip side of this frustration happens when the man comes home from work. You see, most women make a false assumption when they see their husband's body coming in the door. *The woman assumes that her husband came home with his body. But he did not!* He sent his body on ahead to meet the deadline so he wouldn't be badgered all night. But he's not really there. He's *out there somewhere* expanding and developing his business or looking for a deal, but he's not here, in the now.

If your man is out there somewhere, you must tell him that he is home now. I think Marabel Morgan's suggestion in *Total Woman* is a bit excessive. She suggests that you greet your man at the door wearing boots and, well, just boots! I believe most men, when greeted in this manner, would say, "Oh, excuse me!" thinking he had the wrong house! Tell him he's home. Talk about how good it is to be at home with him. Then feed him something. This may be the only clue that your man is able to discern—food! Once you have fed him you are likely to notice an incredible change in him—a change from out there somewhere to living in the now.

POSSESS OR BE POSSESSED?

Earlier in this book I mentioned that man has an inner female and woman has an inner male. If a man possesses (controls) his inner female, he exudes warmth, sensitivity, and healing. But when he is possessed by his inner female, he goes into a strange moodiness. He goes into a passive, withdrawn state, vaguely blaming others for his mood. In this state he is unavailable for relating to people—especially his wife.

When a woman experiences the dark side of her man's inner female, she tries to bail him out of this horrible mood. But this is the absolute worst thing she could do in the midst of his female attack. She now gets rebuffed by her husband because he is unable to relate to her in this state. This triggers the dark side of her inner male, and she has a male attack! She is filled with criticism, judgment, and angry opinions against him. Now there are two people who are possessed by their inner counterpart and in no way capable of relationship. Both man and woman must learn to control their inner capacities for relationship. *Possess yourself or be possessed by yourself.*

When your man is having a female attack, let him have his attack all by himself. There is nothing you can do to help. In the same way, when your woman is having a male attack, do not react against her! Her anger will surely bruise you.

THINKERS AND FEELERS

Understanding maleness and femaleness is a great aid in knowing how to communicate to your mate or other family member. *Most males think first and then feel. Most females feel first and then think.* In light of this, a woman must never ask her man how he feels until she pulls out of him what he thinks. So the first question a woman asks a man must be, "What do you think?" Conversely, a man must never ask a woman what she thinks until after he inquires about how she feels. When this is not followed, women suspect that their husbands have no feelings and men believe that their wives are unable to think.

Both are completely mistaken, because their initial, and possibly total, approach to the opposite sex is all wrong. A simple Biblical principle corrects the perspective. It says: *Let each individual among you also love his own wife even as himself; and let the wife see to it that she respect her husband* (Ephesians 5:33).

According to this and various psychological studies, a man primarily needs respect and a woman primarily needs love or cherishing. Failure in this becomes a vicious cycle. If a woman isn't cherished by her man, she will not respect him. And if a man doesn't get respect, it is very difficult for him to cherish his wife.

A man needs respect but he can easily become bankrupt in this area by two extreme behaviors. The first extreme is to be demanding about it. You can't demand respect, especially by being verbally or physically abusive. Another extreme is to be walking on eggs, playing the part of a wimp. A woman can only respect a man who is a man—responsible and caring.

A woman needs to be cherished. And when she isn't, she becomes increasingly hard and brittle—almost unlovable. She must be careful not to become a "clinging vine," begging her man to cherish her, nor a "bloody Mary," becoming caustic in nagging him toward cherishing. A man can only cherish a woman who is a woman—respectful and supportive.

Man plus woman need not become a ritual. Stress

in the family will be greatly reduced when man and woman *stop role-playing and start relating. Men—control your inner female and cherish your wife. Women—control your inner male and respect your husband.*

CHAPTER 17
Parental Insanity Is Hereditary

Parental insanity is hereditary—you can get it from your kids! Children make a major contribution to the stress in the family. Nobody planned it that way—it just sort of happened.

Probably the most important and valuable task on this earth is "growing" children. It's also one of the most difficult responsibilities. The only thing that children wear out faster than shoes are parents and teachers!

Much has been said about discipline and responsibility, parenting styles and strategies, and the proper spiritual instruction necessary to produce healthy children. Films, books, seminars, and tapes are packed with helpful insights and methods of implementation.

It's amazing how much has been created on the parent-child theme, and yet we don't seem to be winning in reproducing a valuable generation. I believe, as in so many other things, that we are committed to parenting, but not adequately involved. We know what to do, but we just don't do it. Even worse, in most cases, *we are not home long enough to do what we know to do.* One reason why kids are on the streets today may be that they are afraid to stay home—*alone.*

There is one dynamic in parenting that is the most essential of all. Without it, the best discipline and instruction in the world will not win. But with this dynamic, you could blow it in your discipline, possess a lousy parenting style, have no strategy whatsoever, and still win! This dynamic is a *relationship* with your child. You can do nothing effectively until you have it, and you will do nothing that lasts unless you've got it. *Without a relationship with your child you forfeit the right of parenting, because parenting is relationship.*

There are seven vital elements of a relationship.

1. SATISFACTION

Are you satisfied with your child? Do you like who your child is? One mother said to me, "I'm willing to die for my kid, but I really don't like him!"

Are you satisfied with your child's personality? Is he/she too sensitive, too inquisitive, too abrasive?

Are you satisfied with your child physically? You were the big "jock" in school—captain of the football team. But your son can't walk across the room without tripping. Are you satisfied with your child?

What about your child's intellectual ability? You got all A's. At least, that's the way the story goes. Of course, you can't find your report cards and honor certificates anymore, because they were destroyed in the flood. Now your child is making C's, D's, and other such letters! Are you satisfied with him?

I'm not suggesting that you build a monument to mediocrity. Certainly, part of growing up is improving and setting goals for doing even better. But are you satisfied with the makeup of your child—physically, psychologically, and mentally? Does your child know you are satisfied with him/her?

When John McKay was coaching USC football, his son was one of the players. The team and his son were enjoying a super year. I heard the postgame interview with Coach McKay after his son performed especially well. The reporter said, "I'm sure you're proud of your son for playing football so well this year." Coach McKay never skipped a beat in replying, "I'd be proud of my son if he had never played a football game!" The reporter's shock was evident as he fumbled on to the next question!

What Coach McKay was saying is that he was satisfied with his son. Are you? Does your child know that?

2. COMMITMENT

The second element of a relationship is commitment. Are you committed to what your child thinks and feels, and to his interests? To reject a child's interests or feelings is to reject the child.

A desperate father of five boys came in to me concerning his youngest son, who had "mysteriously turned into the black sheep of the family." He said, "My son has gotten deeply involved in a dirty sport—midget racing! He just keeps making weird decisions about his life that don't fit the family. I'm losing my son! What'll I do with him?"

I suggested a first step, knowing that if he bought this one we were on our way to winning. "Get involved in midget racing!" He protested, "But isn't there anything else I can do?" There wasn't. Until his son felt commitment from his dad, nothing else really mattered! So dad jumped into the greasy sport of midget racing.

Just three months later the boy sold his midget racer and chose another interest that he knew his dad wouldn't like. In effect, he was saying, "Dad, you made a good shot by getting involved in midget racing, but let's see how committed you really are!" It's a test of commitment! This dad went through three such tests of commitment before he passed. And you know what? The black sheep turned white!

Another way of demonstrating your commitment is to seek your child's opinions. I didn't say to embrace their opinions, but to value them! Let them help make some family decisions, major and minor. This element of relationship matures children quickly and in a quality way.

When in the third grade, my parents were considering moving from the farm to the city. They carefully brought me into the decision-making process by asking my opinions about the move. It never occurred to me that they could have out voted me 2 to 1. But I was involved in this major decision-making process and greatly appreciated the fact that my parents cared what I thought and felt.

Still another way to show commitment is to listen to your child. Each child needs focused attention. Have you ever wondered how a person can find great help from a local "shrink" who just listens and never offers any counsel? It's because there is something most therapeutic about having someone listen to you. The same is true for your child. He needs your undivided attention in which he has an invitation to express himself. By the way, kids have an uncanny ability to sense whether you really want to hear what they are saying.

Don't con yourself into thinking that quality of time is more important than quantity. Although this statement contains a measure of truth, unless you have quantity time it's nearly impossible to have quality time. Spend the time to express your commitment to your child.

3. TRANSPARENCY

Transparency in a relationship is truthfulness to the point of *vulnerability*. Because of our pride and insecurity, it's very difficult to admit weakness, failure, and unfairness to our children. This is especially true when you have wronged your child.

When you think about it, why is it so important to be vulnerable and admit to your child that you were wrong? Oh, we know it's a good example for them to follow and that it will show them that nobody's perfect. But there is something much more critical than either of these. You see, your child already knows that you were wrong. All he wants to know is, "Do you know that you blew it?" Parents lose most of their credibility right here. It's a major parental cover-up, and it doesn't work!

4. INTIMACY

Intimacy is the element of relationship that treats each child as an individual and not just as part of the group. Part of this intimacy is keeping family matters within the family. Don't share personal things with friends and the neighborhood. I've seen too many kids who have finally reached the point where they feel secure enough to "open up" to mom or dad and then later hear of this intimate, "private" conversation from someone else. If we treated adults with the same respect as we do our children, who would be our friends? It's no wonder kids don't feel like opening up more often!

Another facet of the element of intimacy is that parents must "build the fence but enjoy the pasture areas." Parents build the fence (the boundaries of right and wrong) for the child. If the child breaks out of that fenced area, he must pay the consequences. Inside the boundaries is a pasture area (relational area) to be enjoyed. Many parents, after building the fence, remain outside the pasture area to put out potential fires, to patch the holes, and to generally patrol the area in case the child attempts to break out.

When parents leave their child alone in the pasture area and spend most of their time policing the fence, they become a target for the child. In order for the child to get any relational time, this lonely kid must get mom and dad's attention. What better way to get their attention than to break through the fence? You'll never be able to stop your child from breaking through the fence from time to time. So don't waste your time patrolling the area. Enjoy interrelating with your child within the pasture area, so that when he does break through the fence, he'll have your relationship to draw him back within the proper boundaries.

5. EXPECTANCY

View your child positively. If you see him as a problem, he will fulfill your expectation! We have become very good at labeling our children. These labels serve no useful purpose at all, but seemingly become a sensible goal for the child to fulfill. We say things like "Johnny's the clown of the family." Watch out! It's as if he has just been introduced to come up on stage and perform. And he will!

Expectancy is also giving your child a sense of destiny. A sense of destiny is a sense that God has something special for your child to do in life that no one else can do. It's a view toward a mission in life—a worthwhile contribution by a worthy person.

All my life I heard from my mother the same detailed story about the unusual circumstances which surrounded my birth (no star or angels—just some special happenings!). My mom was pregnant with me when my dad was shipped off to Europe to fight in World War Two. He was shot and imprisoned for a little over four months. The government listed him as "missing in action" and most probably dead.

My mom would not accept the probability that my dad might not return to be a father to me. She wrote nearly 50 letters to people who might know of my dad's dilemma so that she could put the puzzle together piece by piece. She wrote that she had "an unusual confidence that her husband would return home before Jr. was to be born." (I was Jr.!)

At the very same time Dad had written a letter to Mom, but was unable to smuggle it out. He carried it home with him. In this letter Dad said, "I wish you could know the unusual confidence I have that I'll get out of here and be home before Jr. is born!"

My dad returned home on Saturday, May 19, and I showed up on Saturday, May 26! I was a month late, but very much on time! My mom related this story to me on several occasions to remind me that God graciously gave me a father to help launch me into what He wanted me to do. I can still hear her say, "God has something special for you to do. Don't let anything or anyone keep you from it!"

You know what? God has something special for every child to do! Give your child a sense of destiny!

6. PERSEVERANCE

Perseverance is one of the most appropriate elements for parenting because it literally means "hang in there!" If there ever was a theme for parenting, this has to be it. Another way of saying this is "This too will pass!" Perseverance means not keeping score—"That's the third time you've done that this week!" or "That's the fifteenth time you've done that this month!" Don't keep score. Administer appropriate consequences and let each action stand on its own.

Keeping score doesn't allow any breathing room or opportunity for change. The normal terms for the scorekeeper parent are *always* and *never*. These words will kill your child's spirit. "Always" and "never" are the most final judgments you can make. Children who are growing and changing every second need to be encouraged and motivated, not poured into concrete molds.

Perseverance also means being unshockable. Kids are capable of saying and doing the most shocking things. They can say, "I hate you!" Many parents hear these words and die in a pile. Kids love to test every boundary possible, and for some that means this is "shock-mom-night." They love to keep you on the "breaking" edge. But you must remain calm under all circumstances.

A kid is capable of coming home and saying, "Mom, I saw some drugs in the hall today!" If mom goes into a shock syndrome, the child is encouraged to expand and exaggerate the scene—"Yeah, I tried some!" He may have only seen the drugs or thought he saw them. But because of your shock, then he "did" much more! Your shock fans the fire of your child's imagination.

Another facet of perseverance is to separate the offense from the offender. Without this separation your child will feel personal rejection each time you reject his behavior. When my oldest daughter, Tammy, was two years old, she sat on my lap and said, "Daddy doesn't love Tammy when she's naughty, do you, Daddy?" "Oh, no, Tammy, Daddy loves Tammy all the time. I love you when you're good *and* when you're naughty. But I don't like what you do when you're naughty."

Later that year, when Sesame Street introduced a witch as a regular on the program, Tammy said, "Daddy, we don't love witches, do we?" I said, "No, Tammy, we *love* witches. But we don't like what they do!" She got the point! You do not have to love what your child does, but be careful not to allow your dislike and rejection to spill over to your child. *Separate the offense from the offender.*

7. COMPASSION

Although a child may not always act like he wants it, he wants and needs your affection. You must physically demonstrate this affection—a hug, kiss, hand on shoulder, etc. In divorce scenes it's important to counsel the children so that they don't feel responsible for the divorce in any way. When I say, "You know your dad loves you, don't you?" kids repeatedly come back with, "Yeah, he tickles me!" or "He dunks me in the pool!" or "He always wrestles with me!" There is something about touching that communicates your affection in a special way.

Empathizing is another way of expressing compassion. Be careful to appreciate your child's feelings. Don't ignore or belittle him. "You're angry, aren't you?'' ''You're disappointed, aren't you?'' I know of only one feeling the younger kids will not let you appreciate. That's when you say, ''You're tired, aren't you?'' There is *no way* they will admit it, even as they are passing out into oblivion!

Compassion is a sense of giving yourself up for your child.

Do you know where I found these elements of a relationship? All of them are rooted in the great love chapter of the Bible—1 Corinthians 13. In other words, these elements of a relationship are asking more than, ''Do you have a healthy relationship with your child?'' They're really asking, ''Do you love your child?'' If I had asked you that earlier, you most naturally would have said, ''Of course I do!'' But with these nitty-gritty elements of a relationship, I now ask you: *Are you a lover of your child? Does your child know this?* There is nothing more profitable that you can do for your child, nor is there anything else that matters until you develop a love relationship!

CHAPTER 18
How to Live Through It!

A local minister was speaking at the chapel service of a mental institution. Right in the middle of his message an old man stood up and yelled, "Tommyrot! Tommyrot!" He then sat down and remained quiet for the rest of the minister's message.

After the service, the minister asked the director of the institution to explain the action of the man who had interrupted his message. "Oh, don't worry about him. You see, about once a week he wakes up and experiences about 30 seconds of sanity. He was just having one of those moments during your message!"

We all have our moments of sanity—just brief periods of being totally awake and completely sane. It's at these moments that we see life much more clearly and are ready to act more wisely. Now that we have surveyed *stress in the family*, let's get a momentary handle on *how to live through it*.

The strategy for living through it involves four primary relationships. Over and over again studies are demonstrating that *quality relationships are the only universal factors that will definitely alleviate the damaging effects of stress*. It's your choice: *die* within the coldness of loneliness or *live* within the warmth of healthy relationships.

This book is not a theoretical exercise for me, but an account of a real-life struggle and search for some practical answers on how to live through my own personal piles of pressure. There have been times in my life that I almost thrived on pressure, but a couple of years ago I was going through an unusual stress overload. This overload created some physical problems that scared me. It was kind of a "momentary wake-up into sanity" for me. From that awakening, four major steps have evolved as a strategy on how to live through it all. From my study, counseling, and personal experience I recommend these four steps for you.

A DAILY HIGH SUMMIT

The first relational step is a daily high summit with yourself. There are two parts to this summit meeting—physical and spiritual. *Physically*, decide that you will eat right and exercise regularly. Only you can make these decisions. No one can or ought to do this for you.

By listening to everyone else's suggestions and following the latest fads, I have lost at least a ton of weight (over 2000 pounds) and have exercised enough to say I was doing something. But I have remained overweight and out-of-shape for years— basically in a state of nonhealth. There's always someone or something to blame for being unsuccessful in maintaining good health. However, the ultimate control center is *you*. You decide whether you're going to follow through or not. I've offered suggested plans for eating and exercising. Check mine out or set up your own strategy, but do something!

Spiritually, you must also decide to eat right and exercise regularly. Your high summit with yourself is also meeting with God. Right eating and regular exercising on the spiritual level is most important in relieving your stress. Spiritually eating right is feeding upon God and His principles for living.

Spiritually exercising regularly is committing yourself to living these life principles. Since God designed man and the family unit, He is able to make it work best.

The high summit with yourself is really your control center for life. Notice that I suggest a daily high summit meeting. It doesn't have to be long. But it starts with "Good morning, God!" rather than "Good God, it's morning!" The high summit is a time for a fresh awareness of who you are and who God is through Bible study,* prayer, and personal reflections. Some people choose a time after work or late at night. But I have found that early morning is the best for me. At any other time I can be and probably will be interrupted. But I always know where I am and that I will have the least interruptions at 5:30 A.M. or 6 A.M. in the morning. There is very little excuse for not having a high summit meeting at this hour! After a six-month span of actually having a high summit with yourself before God, it can easily become a positive addition. It's an addition to life itself!

A WEEKLY MARITAL SUMMIT

The next-most-important relationship (outside of the high summit with yourself before God) is with your mate. Believe me, this is crucial! If you skip your daily high summit, you only have yourself to contend with. But if you don't spend time with your mate, *you will contend or battle with your mate.* Relationships are difficult enough without a mean-

---

*Don't attempt to be a theologian. Keep it simple. Begin by reading a chapter of the Proverbs which corresponds to the day of the month.

ingful strategy for communication. You need a weekly marital summit.

A weekly marital summit must be a time alone with your mate for at least an hour. I think it's best to tie it together with a "date" night. But you can easily make your summit a luncheon or an after-dinner meeting at home. You must fight for these times together! You must understand that it's better to *fight together* for this time than to fight against each other later!

The weekly marital summit eliminates the frequent arguments that occur over issues. Many arguments are created when one mate has been stewing for a few days about something. Then, after thinking it through thoroughly, he/she springs it on his/her mate and demands an opinion or a decision. A marriage can temporarily come unglued through scenes like this. Very little is accomplished in this haphazard meeting. It's much easier to say, "Let's discuss this at our summit meeting Thursday night." This facilitates quality communication and allows for quality time for decision-making.

A WEEKLY FAMILY COUNCIL

The next priority relationship is the weekly family council. Our family council is normally on Sunday evening. There is always one *must* at our council meeting—*popcorn!* In addition to the appropriate food necessary for the "deep" discussion, we have a 4-D family council!

Dingleberries

Dingleberries are gripes. It's crucial to get any and all out in the open. This is a time for kids to express where they believe parents or another family member has been unfair. It's also a great time for parents to deal with irresponsibility on the part of the children—sloppy room, misuse of phone or car, chores left undone, etc. Whatever the dingleberries, get them out and resolve them. If you can't resolve them immediately, set a time when they can be settled.

Duties

Duties are the responsibilities of each member of the family (parents included). Everyone must share the load. No one is exempt. Everything your child does for himself and for the mutual benefit of the family is a growth experience for him/her. When you do everything for your kids, you cripple their maturity process.

Development

Each family member needs to be engaged in personal development. We encourage our children to have at least two areas of development (sports, music, scouts, etc.).

In addition to these individual areas of development, we are interested in encouraging physical and spiritual development in our children. So we discuss eating right and exercising regularly with some plan of what we will do, individually or as a group.

In the spiritual area we plan good input for our kids. We have planned six types of spiritual input for our kids:

1. Sunday school.
2. Early morning Bible study, and prayer as a family.

3. Periodic reading to them in the evening.

4. Kid's club—a weekly Bible study in our neighborhood.

5. Family council—we discuss some principle of life, something we think they need to know (how to respond when insulted, how to develop a friend, giving, etc.).

6. We also make sure that our kids get the quality input of summer camps and youth retreats where they will receive healthy guidance by quality counselors.

Decisions

Include your children in as many of your family decisions as you possibly can, major or minor. Get them involved in helping to plan the family vacation. They will enjoy it much more, and therefore you will enjoy it more!

Also, take a look at the calendar together and plan some play time together. Draw out of them the kinds of things they want to do as a family. Be a good sport and try it all.

Another area of decisions and planning is special events. Special events include holidays, birthdays, and other family celebrations. These are the kinds of decisions that create family traditions and family unity.

A REGULAR GROWTH GROUP

The final, strategic relational step to alleviate your stress overload is to get involved in a growth group. A growth group is an extended family relationship. It's a positive relational experience with other people outside your immediate family.

A growth group provides a relational context in which you can engage yourself. It's a group where you support one another, and cry together. It's a group where your children find a warm hand of encouragement from another significant adult. This communicates to your child that he/she is a significant person.

Growth groups can be experienced in almost any setting. Some find this experience through Bible study groups, minichurch groups, or neighborhood groups. These groupings will change from year to year because your activities normally change that way. Sell whatever you must to belong to a caring growth group. It rounds out your relational needs for a buffer against negative stress overload.

Any of these steps will help you alleviate the stress in your life, but all four steps will insure that you are doing all that you can do to process the pressure. I love the Biblical passage that speaks to physical and spiritual discipline:

Have nothing to do with worldly fables, but discipline yourself for the purpose of godliness [wise living according to God's principles]; for bodily discipline is only of little profit [but it is profitable], but godliness [discipline] is profitable for all things, since it holds promise for the present life and also for the life to come. . . . For it is for this we labor and strive, because we have fixed our hope on the living God, who is the Savior of all men, especially of believers (1 Timothy 4:7,8,10).

Three people—a priest, a Boy Scout, and a computer executive—were passengers in an ill-equipped small plane from Los Angeles to Fresno. As Murphy would have it, ill-equipped small planes will inevitably need their missing or broken equipment.

The plane developed engine trouble, and there

was no doubt that they were going to crash. As soon as the pilot realized their doom, he stood up and announced, "We're going to crash soon, and there are only three parachutes. I have a young family who needs me desperately, so I'm taking one of these parachutes for me!" He picked up one of the parachutes and jumped!

The computer executive immediately stood up and said, "I have been called by some the smartest man in all the world. If I were to go down with this plane, it would be such a loss to computer science. I'm taking a parachute and jumping! Good luck!" He grabbed another chute and jumped out of the plane.

The priest said to the Boy Scout, "Son, I'm old and ready to meet my Maker. You're so young, with most of your life ahead of you. You take that last parachute and save yourself!" The Boy Scout replied, "Calm down, Father, the smartest man in all the world just grabbed my knapsack and jumped out of the plane!"

Life is like that—We all must jump. Every decision is a jump. We can go down with either a parachute or a knapsack. Some of the smartest people in all the world choose the knapsack. Which will you choose? Go down with a knapsack and you'll hit with a thud. Go down with a parachute and you'll surely live through it!

CHAPTER NOTES

INTRODUCTION

1. Kenneth R. Pelletier, "Mind As Healer, Mind As Slayer," *Psychology Today,* February 1977, p. 35.
2. Dave Stoop, *Self Talk* (Old Tappan, NJ: Fleming H. Revell Co., 1982), p. 13.
3. Ibid.
4. Ibid.
5. Gary Collins, *You Can Profit From Stress* (Santa Ana, CA: Vision House, 1977), p. 13.
6. Cecil Osborne, *Release from Fear and Anxiety* (Waco, TX: Word Books, 1976), p. 15.
7. Ibid.
8. Ibid., p. 16.
9. Merle Shain, *When Lovers Are Friends* (New York: Bantam Books, 1978), pp. 16-17, 22-23.
10. Ibid., p. 30.
11. "Role of Young Adults in the Years Ahead," *U.S. News and World Report,* May 27, 1978, p. 62.
12. Ibid.

CHAPTER 1
YOUR BODY'S CHARGE ACCOUNT

1. Karl Albrecht, *Stress and the Manager* (Englewood Cliffs, NJ: Spectrum Book), p. 53.
2. Hans Selye, *The Stress of Life,* (New York: McGraw-Hill, 1976), p. 32.
3. Albrecht, *Stress and the Manager,* pp. 53-55.
4. Ibid.
5. George Everly and Daniel Girdano, *Controlling Stress and Tension* (Englewood Cliffs, NJ: Prentice-Hall, 1979), p. 222.
6. Ibid., p. 69.
7. Keith W. Sehnert, *Stress/Unstress* (Minneapolis: Augsburg Publishing House, 1981), pp. 64, 74-75.
8. Ibid., p. 66.
9. Albrecht, *Stress and the Manager,* p. 69.

CHAPTER 2
STRESS IS IN THE HEAD

1. Wayne Dyer, *Your Erroneous Zones* (New York: Funk and Wagnalls, 1976), p. 20.
2. Tim Timmons, *Maximum Living in a Pressure-cooker World* (Waco, TX: Word Books, 1979), p. 15.
3. Dennis Jaffe, *Healing From Within* (New York: Knopf Publications, 1980), p. 6.
4. Ibid., p. 8.
5. Kenneth R. Pelletier, *Mind As Healer, Mind As Slayer* (New York: A Delta Book, 1981), p. 20.
6. Ruth Maxwell, *The Booze Battle: A Common Sense Approach That Works* (New York: Praeger Publishers, 1976).
7. Pelletier, *Mind As Healer*, p. 317.

CHAPTER 3
THE BODY LANGUAGE OF STRESS

1. Ann Aikman and Walter McQuade, *Stress* (New York: Bantam Books, 1981), pp. 5-6.
2. Pelletier, *Mind As Healer*, p. 6.
3. Sehnert, *Stress/Unstress*, p. 161.
4. William Dufty, *Sugar Blues* (New York: Warner Books, 1975), pp. 46-47.
5. Pelletier, *Mind As Healer*, p. 86.
6. Ibid., pp. 15-16.
7. Ibid., p. 158.
8. Meyer Friedman and Ray Rosenman, *Type A: Behavior and Your Heart* (New York: Knopf, 1974).
9. Aikman and McQuade, *Stress*, p. 24.
10. Pelletier, *Mind As Healer*, p. 91.
11. Ibid., p. 159.
12. Aikman and McQuade, *Stress*, p. 24.
13. Ibid., pp. 40-41.
14. Ibid., pp. 55-56.
15. Ibid., pp. 62-68.
16. Ibid., p. 68.
17. Ibid., p. 73.

18. Jaffe, *Healing From Within*, p. 92.
19. Pelletier, *Mind As Healer*, pp. 134-35.
20. Aikman and McQuade, *Stress*, p. 82.

CHAPTER 4
PEOPLE PRESSURE

1. M. Pflanz, E. Rosenstein, and T. Von Uexkull, *Journal of Psychosomatic Research*, Feb. 1956, pp. 68-74.
2. Everly and Girdano, *Controlling Stress and Tension*, p. 74.
3. Tim Timmons, *Loneliness Is Not a Disease* (Eugene, OR: Harvest House, 1981), pp. 55-58.
4. Ibid.
5. Ibid.
6. Ibid.
7. Albrecht, *Stress and the Manager*, p. 8.
8. Ibid., pp. 9-10.
9. Ibid., p. 10.
10. Ibid., pp. 16-17.
11. Ibid., pp. 21-22.
12. Ibid., p. 9.
13. Sehnert, *Stress/Unstress*, pp. 32-33.
14. Albrecht, *Stress and the Manager*, p. 16.
15. Ibid., p. 23.
16. Jaffe, *Healing From With.... n*, p. 147.

CHAPTER 5
LITTLE PEOPLE UNDER PRESSURE

1. David Elkind, *The Hurried Child* (Reading, MA: Addison-Wesley Publishing Co., 1982), p. 25.
2. U.S. Department of Commerce, 1980.
3. Elkind, *The Hurried Child*, pp. 26-27.
4. *Parent's* Magazine, "What T.V. is Doing To Your Kids," June 1981.
5. *U.S. News & World Report*, Jan. 19, 1981, p. 45.
6. Ibid.
7. Ibid.

8. Ibid.
9. Ibid.
10. Elkind, *The Hurried Child,* p. 83.
11. Ibid., p. 86.
12. Ibid., p. 88.
13. Everly and Girdano, *Controlling Stress and Tension,* pp.
14. 73-74.
    Newsweek, Feb. 16, 1981, p. 51.
15. Elkind, *The Hurried Child,* pp. 150-51.
16. Ibid., pp. 149-50.
17. *Newsweek,* Aug. 9, 1982, p. 45.
18. Ibid.
19. Ibid.
20. Ibid.
21. Ibid.
22. Pelletier, *Mind As Healer,* p. 142.
23. *Toronto Star,* Sept. 3, 1980.

CHAPTER 6
THE BATTLE OF THE SEXES

1. James Neely, *Gender* (New York: Simon & Schuster, 1981),
   p. 41.
2. Pat Allen, *Conversational Rape* (Newport Beach, CA: Want
   Training, pp. 68-69).
3. Morton Kelsey, *Caring* (New York: Paulist Press, 1981), p.
   110.
4. Pierre Mornell, *Passive Men, Wild Women* (New York:
   Simon & Schuster, 1979).
5. Neely, *Gender,* p. 72.

CHAPTER 7
YOUR "LITTLE KID" IS SHOWING!

1. W. Hugh Missildine, *Your Inner Child of the Past* (New
   York: Pocket Books, 1963), p. 3.
2. Ibid.

3. Ibid.
4. Grace Kirsten and Richard Robertiello, *Big You, Little You* (New York: Pocket Books, 1975), p. 24.
5. Ibid.
6. Ibid., p. 33.
7. Ibid., p. 84.
8. Missildine, *Inner Child,* p. 286.
9. Ibid., pp. 289-290.

CHAPTER 8
THE ULTIMATE SOURCE OF STRESS—MURPHY!

1. Jeremy Rifkin, *Entropy* (New York: The Viking Press, 1980), p. 3.
2. Ibid.
3. Ibid., p. 4.
4. Ibid., p. 6.
5. Ibid., p. 34.
6. William Ophuls, *Ecology and the Politics of Scarcity* (San Francisco: Freeman Publishing, 1977), p. 87.
7. "Our Population Predicament: A New Look," Population Reference Bureau, Inc., vol. 34, no. 5, Dec. 1979.
8. Jacques Ellul, *The Technological Society* (New York: Random House, 1964), p. 105.
9. Rifkin, *Entropy,* p. 81.
10. Christopher Lasch, *The Culture of Narcissism* (New York: W.W. Norton & Co., Inc., 1978), p. 27.

CHAPTER 10
LEARNING TO BE A LOVER

1. Ed Wheat, *Love Life* (Grand Rapids: Zondervan, 1980), p. 57.
2. John Powell, *The Secret of Staying in Love* (Chicago: Argus Communications, 1974), p. 55.
3. Ibid., p. 56.
4 . Lewis B. Smedes, *Love Without Limits* (Grand Rapids: Wm.

B. Eerdmans, 1978), pp. 1, 11.
5. Powell, *Secret,* p. 53.
6. Ibid., pp. 69-70.

CHAPTER 13
LIVING LIFE ON PURPOSE

1. Alan Lakein, *U.S. News & World Report,* Jan. 19, 1976.
2. Udo Middlemann, *Pro-Existence* (Downers Grove, IL: InterVarsity Press, 1974), p. 27.
3. Ibid., pp. 18-19.

CHAPTER 15
MIND YOUR OWN LIFE

1. Melvin Page and H. Leon Abrams, Jr., *Your Body Is Your Best Doctor* (New Canaan, CT: Keats Publishing, Inc., 1976), p. 54.
2. Harvey Diamond, *The Totally Healthy Person* (Santa Monica, CA: Golden Glow Publishers, 1979), pp. 204-5.
3. Ibid.
4. Ibid.
5. Ibid.
6. Ibid.
7. Ibid.
8. Nathan Pritikin, *The Pritikin Program* (New York: Bantam Books, 1981), pp. 71-72.
9. James J. Lynch, *The Broken Heart* (New York: Basic Books, Inc., 1977), p. 160.
10. William Glasser, *The Identity Society* (New York: Harber & Row, 1976), pp. 55-56.
11. Ibid., p. 57.
12. Ira J. Tanner, *Loneliness: The Fear of Love* (New York: Harper & Row, 1973), p. XI.
13. Ibid., pp. 79-80.
14. Ibid., p. 36.
15. Ibid., p. 12.
16. Clark E. Moustakas, *Loneliness and Love* (Englewood Cliffs, NJ: Prentice Hall, Inc., 1972), pp. 143-45.

17. Tanner, *Loneliness: The Fear of Love*, p. X.
18. Moustakas, *Loneliness and Love*, p. 87.
19. Clark E. Moustakas, *The Touch of Loneliness* (Englewood Cliffs, NJ: Prentice Hall, Inc., 1975), pp. 77-78.
20. Tanner, *Loneliness: The Fear of Love*, p. 71.
21. John Powell, *Why Am I Afraid to Love?* (Chicago: Argus Communications, 1972), pp. 23-24.

CHAPTER 16
WOMEN ARE WEIRD AND
MEN ARE STRANGE

1. Daniel Yankelovich, *New Rules* (New York: Random House, 1981).